THE

GRASSROOTS
HEALTH CARE
REVOLUTION

"This is the playbook for employers who want to control costs while improving care for their employees. John Torinus, Serigraph, and other leading-edge companies show what's possible by being bold and applying common sense strategies to health-benefit management. If enough employers followed suit, they'd change the market while getting better results for their employees and their companies."

—Cheryl DeMars,
CEO of The Alliance

"As John Torinus points out, for most CEOs, health care is the second or third largest element of their cost structure—and generally the most undermanaged significant cost. His new book lays out a three-year transition from unmanaged health care to a health system that provides dramatically improved participant health with dramatically reduced costs."

—George Koenigsaecker,
author of *Leading the Lean Enterprise Transformation*

"The 2,700-page Patient Protection and Affordable Care Act was signed into law by President Obama on March 23, 2010. As the law approaches its fourth anniversary, it is clear that the United States will achieve neither lower costs nor universal coverage under this plan. Instead, Obamacare increases the role of the federal government in our health care system which will lead to long waits, rationed care, and a lack of access to the latest technology and treatments for all of us. In order to achieve affordable, accessible, quality care for all Americans, we need a system that empowers doctors and patients and awards innovation. In his new book, *The Grassroots Health Care Revolution: How Companies Across America Are Dramatically Cutting Their Health Care Costs While Improving Care*, John Torinus shows through his many interviews with employers and employees how a patient-centric model of reform is the solution to what ails our system. This book is a must read."

—SALLY C. PIPES,
President and CEO of the Pacific Research Institute
and author of *The Cure for Obamacare*

"John Torinus has been experimenting with improving health care cost and quality in his company for over a decade. His work at Serigraph Inc. in Wisconsin clearly shows employers can radically reduce the total cost of health care benefits while still maintaining employee choice. Torinus succinctly explains how employers anywhere can offer great health care benefits at much less cost. This is a must read for any leader struggling to manage their health care costs."

—JOHN TOUSSAINT,
CEO of Center for Valued Based Healthcare

PRAISE FOR JOHN TORINUS
AND *THE COMPANY THAT SOLVED HEALTH CARE*

"John Torinus is a national treasure. Every business can learn from what he did at Serigraph."

—REGINA E. HERZLINGER,
Nancy R. McPherson Professor of Business Administration
at the Harvard Business School, author of *Who Killed Health Care?*

"The health care industry is badly in need of new business models and systems thinking. *The Company That Solved Health Care* incorporates some of the best management disciplines as it proves health and health care costs can be improved dramatically at the ground level."

—PAUL O'NEILL,
former CEO of Alcoa and Secretary of the Treasury

"Torinus has sought out the best innovators in Wisconsin for delivering more value in health care, and he put them to work at Serigraph. His company has proved that purchasers of health care can manage their costs and control their destiny far more effectively than 'command and control' government approaches. He has pushed the industry hard to improve, and it has helped us get better. His prescription is on the mark."

—STEVE BRENTON,
President, Wisconsin Hospital Association

"While much of the country is focused on the attempts to reform health care in Washington, there is a revolution going on under their noses. This book describes the real-world revolution that is transforming health care into a cost-efficient, accountable system through empowering consumers. John Torinus is no dreamer. He shows us how his company has walked the walk and actually made it happen. This is must-reading for every employer who is concerned about staying in business in a difficult economy."

—GREG SCANDLEN,
Editor, *Consumer Power Report*

"Manitowoc County took a page directly out of the innovations for managing health care costs spearheaded by John Torinus at Serigraph, and it worked. We convinced our non-represented employees and six employee bargaining units to work with us in making these changes, putting millions of dollars into the pockets of our four hundred employees while capturing significant savings for taxpayers. Consumer-driven health care changes EVERYTHING!"

—BOB ZIEGELBAUER,
Wisconsin State Representative (D)
and Manitowoc (WI) County Executive

"Torinus has succinctly chronicled the remarkable success at Serigraph in controlling company health care costs. This story serves as evidence to U.S. employers and the government that it's possible to bend the health care expense curve. His prescription? Work with employees to help them become better consumers by providing price and quality data on doctors, hospitals, and prescription drugs so they can take responsibility for their own health, and by creating benefit incentives that encourage the right behaviors. This isn't academic theory. Torinus has made it work."

—JOHN TOUSSAINT,
CEO, ThedaCare Center for Healthcare Value

"Prevention, wellness, and chronic disease management have to be foremost if the nation is going to dramatically improve health and significantly lower costs of care. Serigraph's business model proves those initiatives work in a very real way. The book is a must for every business as it deals with health care."

—TOMMY THOMPSON,
former Governor of Wisconsin and
Former U.S. Secretary of Health and Human Services

"Anyone hoping to sit quietly on the sidelines until John Torinus tires of his campaign to change health care in our country would do well to remember that John rode his bike across America at age 71 and skis through the hilly and frigid course of the American Birkebeiner. John brings the focus and energy of an endurance athlete to his work to keep his company competitive by changing the way we buy and, more importantly, think about health care.

Since I met John in 1996, he has been an active participant in health reform debates and a relentless voice for change. We were at the table together when a small group of Wisconsin providers started down that path of transparency as part of the Wisconsin Collaborative for Health Care Quality. Those initial steps were a leap of faith as providers began to share quality and cost data with customers and each other. This work set a path for larger initiatives, like the Wisconsin Hospital Association's Price Point and Check Point. Wisconsin is now considered a national leader, due in some measure to that early work.

His book offers the reader a bird's-eye view of the changes and innovations John shepherded at Serigraph. Like all good innovators, John keeps experimenting and has hits and misses. While I am not in total agreement with all that John has proposed for his workers (for example, I share his co-workers' skepticism about medical tourism), clearly his focus on staff engagement is key to any health reform effort. This is a critical point whether at the work area or in the national reform agenda. His prescription offers insights into the winning strategy of empowering individuals to take an active role in managing their health. The focus on wellness, prevention, and end-of-life planning yield more impressive benefits than cost savings: some of John's co-workers will no doubt live longer and live better because they were offered the right incentives and support to catch disease early or take steps to prevent it altogether.

John and I will continue to debate and argue over the best methods for lowering overall costs in the years ahead, but John's heart is in the right direction. What he is looking for is what every CEO should be focusing on—how do we improve the health status of our workers while improving the cost and quality of health care services. I look forward to the thought-provoking discussions, and his readers will enjoy a thought-provoking book."

—WILLIAM D. PETASNICK,
President and CEO, Froedtert & Community Health and
Former Chair of the American Hospital Association

"Serigraph's focus, organizational commitment, and collaboration with its health plan administrator, Anthem Blue Cross and Blue Shield, and providers of value in health care proves that there are innovative solutions for getting the hyper-inflation in health care under control. It's not a blame game; it's about individual engagement, transparency, and effective management."

—STEVE MARTENET,
President of WellPoint Specialty Products and
Former President of Anthem Blue Cross and Blue Shield in Wisconsin

How Companies Across America
Are Dramatically Cutting Their Health Care Costs
While Improving Care

THE

GRASSROOTS
HEALTH CARE
REVOLUTION

John Torinus Jr.

BENBELLA BOOKS, INC.
DALLAS, TEXAS

BenBella

BenBella Books, Inc.
10030 N. Central Expressway, Suite 530
Dallas, TX 75231
www.benbellabooks.com
Send feedback to feedback@benbellabooks.com

Printed in the United States of America
10 9 8 7 6 5 4 3 2 1

Library of Congress Cataloging-in-Publication Data

Torinus, John, Jr., author.
    The grassroots health care revolution : how companies across America are dramatically cutting their health care costs while improving care / by John Torinus.
        p. ; cm.
    Includes bibliographical references and index.
    ISBN 978-1-939529-72-5 (trade cloth : alk. paper)—ISBN 978-1-939529-73-2 (electronic)
    I. Title.
    [DNLM: 1. Health Benefit Plans, Employee—economics—United States. 2. Costs and Cost Analysis—economics—United States. 3. Health Care Reform—economics—United States. 4. National Health Insurance, United States—economics—United States. W 275 AA1]
    RA412.3
    368.38'2—dc23
                                                                  2013041457

Editing by Debbie Harmsen
Proofreading by Rainbow Graphics and Greg Teague
Cover design by Ted Mauseth
Jacket design by Sarah Dombrowsky
Text design and composition by John Reinhardt Book Design
Printed by Bang Printing

Distributed by Perseus Distribution
(www.perseusdistribution.com)

To place orders through Perseus Distribution:
Tel: 800-343-4499
Fax: 800-351-5073
E-mail: orderentry@perseusbooks.com

Significant discounts for bulk sales are available.
Please contact Glenn Yeffeth at glenn@benbellabooks.com or 214-750-3628.

The march is on to a new business model for the delivery of health care in America. Actually, it is a race. This book is dedicated to the innovators, most of whom are in the private sector, who are putting the pieces into place for that disruptive model. Health costs are the biggest economic issue facing the country. So these innovators—many are featured in this book—are doing patriotic work. They are fixing a broken, unsustainable model.

CONTENTS

INTRODUCTION

TWO ENTIRELY DIFFERENT mind-sets are at work in the world of U.S. health care. The public and private sectors, which roughly split the nation's nearly $3 trillion medical bill, see different challenges. Government leaders think reform means more access for more people through better insurance, subsidies, and expanded tax revenues; private companies see out-of-control costs as the main issue and improved workforce health as a major solution. The health care law that was signed into law in 2010 and has begun taking effect (with the full effect hitting companies in 2015) is all about access and insurance reform, but it leaves largely unaddressed the pivotal issue of costs, which have been spiraling upward for decades. The costs have about doubled every eight years.

In my first book, *The Company That Solved Health Care*, I described what my mid-size manufacturing company, Wisconsin-based Serigraph Inc., did to loosen the cost noose that kept tightening around our neck. Since then, I have had the rewarding experience of traveling the country

1

to interact with hundreds, even thousands, of business people who were also grappling with that huge issue. I got more than I gave. It was a learning journey.

Growing up in the newspaper and manufacturing businesses, with a grandfather in each, I always had one foot in journalism and the other in commerce. Curiosity and questioning are the requisites for a news reporter, and benchmarking on best practices at other companies is an invaluable tool for running a company. Both skills helped as I engaged in a cross-country dialogue with smart people who are passionate about finding a cure for the chaos in health care economics.

As I spoke with businesspeople across the country, it became clear that I am far from the only one who sees that the business side of health care is badly broken. I imparted what we had learned at Serigraph, as we improved workforce health sharply and kept our costs about 40 percent below the national average. But the more interactions I had, the more I realized something profound was taking shape across the land. Collectively, these innovators were hammering out a new business model for the delivery of care.

I, with help from a seasoned business reporter, interviewed many of these change agents, these disrupters, and their insights are spread throughout the book.

The payer revolt has been growing from the ground up, just the opposite of what happened in 2010 when President Obama and Congress imposed insurance reform from the top down. ObamaCare, love it or hate it, was fashioned cerebrally by wonks and pols from inside the Beltway and inside the health care industry. It was anything but empirical, as its troubled launch demonstrated.

ObamaCare, love it or hate it, was fashioned cerebrally by wonks and pols from inside the Beltway and inside the health care industry. It was anything but empirical, as its troubled launch demonstrated.

What I was touching and seeing across America is the "real reform" that has been going on in the private sector at the grassroots level. The innovators have been dealing with the elephant in the room—the bloated cost structure of the industry. They also have been dealing with the health of employees, because you can't manage health costs without managing health. Duh! That basic truth became perfectly obvious in my many conversations.

It should come as no surprise that most of the innovators I encountered were in the private sector. Government payers move very slowly, except to devise new revenue schemes to cover the soaring medical costs. Conversely, innovation is at the heart of survival and competitiveness in the private economy. And corporate executives move fast once they engage a strategic issue and understand that it has to be solved. We in business are a community of problem solvers. We thrive on innovation. And we're motivated to innovate in health care, since we're directly footing roughly half of the bill in this country.

Business leaders can push their reforms with the knowledge that we possess lots of leverage. As Jeff Thompson, CEO of Gundersen Health System in Wisconsin, put it: "All of the margin in health care comes from private payers."

Further, innovators in the private sector are more pragmatic than wonky. They are empirical. They get an idea for improvement, try it, keep it if it works, and dump it if it doesn't. When their proven initiatives and pilots are stitched together, they add up to a new model. It is a mosaic. In contrast, ObamaCare avoids, for the most part, the over-riding issue of costs. So no one really knows if ObamaCare is going to work without busting the bank. And it may not even resolve the access issue. We'll know in five to ten years.

We private payers, on the other hand, know beyond a doubt that the emerging business model in the private sector works, because it is being rolled out successfully in thousands of results-oriented companies.

The emerging business model in the private sector works... it is being rolled out successfully in thousands of results-oriented companies.

Corporate purchasers also understand basic business concepts, like the rock-hard fact that they and their employees are the customers.

Medical providers, who often think they are at the center of their universe, have a hard time with the concept of customer. I often have to explain to them that the customer is the one who writes the check.

Corporate purchasers see the world through supply chains, with the payer at the top and the doctors, hospitals, clinics, and insurers as vendors down the chain. With that mentality, proper relationships start falling into place.

In my learning expeditions, I encountered a mountain of frustration, even anger, at the existing system for delivering care. Most of the ire is on the economic side of the equation, though there is plenty of room for improvement on the medical side.

The American people are fully aware that unchecked health costs—almost twice per capita of anywhere else in the world—are crowding out advances in education, research and development, wage increases, public safety, environmental improvement, even defense. They see the hits to their personal finances. Health costs have become the leading cause of personal bankruptcy in the country. The citizenry wants it fixed.

Fortunately, there is a grassroots revolution surging across the country, company by company, and it offers hope and change. In that light, this is an optimistic book.

The rate of inflation in health care premiums has dropped from double-digit increases a decade ago to mid-single digits. The wonks are puzzled by that unprecedented drop. How did it happen? Look no further than the Grassroots Revolution led by private payers. They are demanding change, and they are making it happen.

This book lays out the initiatives that many companies have launched and the platforms they have built for a restructured health system.

Unlike the current system that revolves around specialist doctors, hospitals, and insurers, the new model centers on the employee, the consumer. The new delivery model listens first to the voice of the customer. It is patient-centric.

That's the heart of what I learned from the innovators at the ramparts of real health care reform, and it's at the heart of this solutions-oriented management book.

1

Go or No-Go
Under ObamaCare?

WITH MAJOR CHUNKS of the new health care law taking effect in 2014 and 2015, companies across the country have been faced with a decision on whether to continue their health benefit, to begin coverage, or to pay federal fines.

On its face, this may not seem like a very involved decision. After all, if companies have been offering health care to employees, why wouldn't they continue to do so? Yet, the new law offers an escape hatch of sorts. It might look like it's cheaper for a company to pay the new fines than provide insurance for each employee. But there's a lot more to the decision.

The new law, above all else, is complicated, and those complications spill over to private companies. Even with the new law, though, the real issue remains the underlying costs, which is why the name of the legislation—the Affordable Care Act—is so ironic. Health care has been many things, but affordable is not among them, and everyone agrees that the new law will not change that reality, that ACA will actually add costs. The only debate is over how much.

The escalating costs are the primary reason companies are faced with the go or no-go decision under ObamaCare. If costs were low, like they were after World War II when companies first got into offering a health care benefit, the decision would be less difficult. No economist is predicting that general cost escalation will lessen in the future.

So, should businesses default to the government exchanges created under ACA to avoid the financial burden of health benefits, or should they stay in the health care game?

This book focuses on ways companies across the country have innovated to reduce health care costs so they can maintain the benefit. It profiles innovators—company by company at the ground level—to describe a rapidly emerging business model for health care. It is a disruptive new model that will force radical change in the way providers and health insurers operate.

Even deeper, at the very root of the national problem, is necessary behavior change by individual employees, as they become engaged consumers. The new model is based on individual responsibility.

Yet while costs and improved health are at the center of the reform in the private sector, no company can ignore the impact of the Patient Protection and Affordable Care Act, also known as ObamaCare or ACA. The decision on whether or not to offer health care for employees is made difficult by the complex, unclear, and still developing rules to flesh out the law. Businesses got a one-year reprieve when the Obama administration moved the effective date of the mandate on employers to provide care or face a penalty from January 1, 2014 to January 1, 2015. But that doesn't change the need to make a fundamental decision on whether to offer health care as a benefit.

THE CHANGING LANDSCAPE OF HEALTH CARE

The percentage of employers that provide a health plan has been dropping steadily over the last several decades. Hyperinflation (a justifiable term) of medical costs has driven 40 percent of U.S. companies, mostly smaller firms, out of coverage. That's down nine points since 2000. No one really knows how many more employers will drop coverage because of soaring medical expenses or because of the new law. But some will, because they haven't figured out how to manage or afford ever-higher premiums.

If a company with 50 or more employees decides to offer health care coverage, it will use either a self-insured plan or a plan sold by an insurance company that meets two ACA tests: 1) it can't cost more than 9.5 percent of an employee's pay, and 2) the employer coverage must pay at least 60 percent of the employee's health care bill.

There are many insurance plans with medium to high deductibles, offset by personal health accounts, that can meet those hurdles. However, for those crunching the numbers, it's a little like shooting in the dark, because no one really knows how much premiums will jump in the years following enactment of the new law. If you can't fix a premium cost, you can't do the percentages.

Most analysts agree, though, that the addition of people with highly expensive pre-existing conditions and other mandates can only drive premium costs upward.

The Obama administration had already pushed back the website startup for small businesses to purchase insurance on the new public exchanges from 2014 policies to 2015. That was a broken promise to those employers that have seen the biggest premium hikes in recent years and were hoping the exchanges might give them some relief. Many extended the small group policies as 2013 came to a close. That bought them a 12-month reprieve to see how prices will shake out for 2015.

SMALL COMPANIES WILL GAME THE RULES

Congress gave small companies a break in the new law. Businesses with fewer than 50 full-time equivalent employees escape the ACA penalties for not providing coverage. That means many small companies will game the rules to stay below 50. They will:

- Choose not to grow
- Adopt labor-saving methods like automation
- Outsource work
- Buy rather than make components
- Split a company into separate corporations to get below the maximum
- Keep part-time employee hours under 30 hours per week so they can't be counted in the full-time equivalent totals

They are already taking those steps in anticipation of the activation of the new law.

The penalty is a slap on the wrist compared to health benefit costs.

Some financially strapped companies with more than 50 employees will be relieved to pay the ACA penalty of only $2,000 per employee as they retreat from a benefit plan that includes health care. The penalty is a slap on the wrist compared to health benefit costs.

THOSE SAYING "GO" TO HEALTH CARE: MOSTLY MEDIUM AND LARGE COMPANIES

My guesstimate is that at least half of the employers in America will make a decision to stay in the health care business, down from 60 percent that offered a health

UNINTENDED CONSEQUENCES LOOMING UNDER OBAMACARE

Premium Hikes—Most states will see premium increases, ranging from low to high, with different impacts on different subsets of people. Political spin on the level of the increases will confuse Americans.

Some Employers Will Drop Plans—At penalties of only $2,000 per full-time worker, firms with high employee turnover will pay the penalty and send their workers to Medicaid or the exchanges.

50-Employee Max—Small firms will do somersaults to stay under the 50-employee limit and avoid ACA penalties.

30-Hour Employees—Companies are managing part-time hours aggressively to avoid the health care mandate that kicks in at 30 hours per week.

Young Healthies Will Fly Naked—Young adults will pay the small penalty and sign up for guaranteed health insurance only when they get sick.

Insurers Won't Play—Major health insurers have decided not to offer individual policies on some state exchanges. That spells limited choices of carriers, often duopolies or oligopolies. Many available health plans on the exchanges will offer narrow networks, which means some hospitals, clinics, and doctors won't be accessible.

Reduced Benefits—Many plans will cut back to avoid the 40 percent Cadillac tax.

Doctor Shortages—Workforce experts predict huge shortages of physicians by 2020 because of the increased demand.

benefit in 2013. Polls confirm that most large and medium employers will continue coverage, and brokers that each represent hundreds of companies, medium and large, also report that almost all of their clients intend to stay the course in offering a health care benefit.

Some have decided, though, to retreat to a defined contribution, say $5,000 to $7,000, where employees will get a check and will be asked to go to the exchanges to buy individual health policies. How big that trend will be remains to be seen.

TYPICAL ARE THE QUOTED COMMENTS of Randy Baker, president of Joy Global's surface mining division: "It is certainly a large line item in our budget, but we are going to continue to offer health care at our company regardless of what the federal government wants to do, because our employees deserve that."

My company reached a similar conclusion. After a rigorous analysis, Serigraph Inc., which self-insures about 1,100 lives, made its decision in 2013 to keep its full health plan, mainly because we cannot afford to lose talented employees if we drop coverage. Some would surely look elsewhere for work at companies with full benefits. There are several such soft costs involved in dropping coverage, and they offset the hard costs of continuing coverage. The competitive reality, at least for now, is that providing coverage for employees is still considered the norm for mid-size and large corporations.

THE COSTS OF HEALTH CARE

Companies that have done the best job of managing the health of their workforces and, therefore, of controlling medical costs, will be the ones most likely to keep their health care benefits. Best-practice employers in the private sector deliver health care for a total cost between $8,000 and $10,000 per employee. That has been and will continue to be a bearable level of expense for companies that want to attract and retain talented employees.

Companies that have done the best job of managing the health of their workforces and, therefore, of controlling medical costs, will be the ones most likely to keep their health care benefits.

Employers who haven't applied management disciplines to health care often pay more than $20,000 per year. At that level, the small penalties under ObamaCare for dropping coverage, $2,000 per employee, look like an easy way out. In short, the higher the costs of a plan, the more likely the company is to drop coverage and pay the penalties for not offering coverage.

The "Cadillac plans," those that cost more than $27,500 for a family, face a 40 percent surtax under ACA, effective 2018. Those bloated plans cover some executives, many union members, and some public employees. They show how far out-of-control costs can climb if not managed. Assuming an 8 percent upward trend in premiums, more than 50 percent of plans could face the 40 percent tax within a decade. Employers will only escape the penalty if they redesign their plans or Congress yields to pressures to raise the cap. Companies are already trimming back their plans in anticipation of 2018.

SOFT COSTS

The proposed rules are maddeningly complex, and thus the decision to stay with health care or drop coverage has been complicated. For openers, the soft costs are as vexing as the hard costs. For exempt smaller companies, among the soft costs are legal fees. They are hiring lawyers and benefits experts to make sure they stay exempt at fewer than 50 employees. The new law has created an army of consultants.

For medium and large employers, the soft costs of discontinuing the health benefit go beyond turnover, but that is the biggest one. Another major one is the loss of influence over promoting health among employers.

If a company drops coverage and instead chooses to pay the modest ACA penalties, what's the cost of losing a top engineer who leaves for a position with a full-benefit employer? Turnover brings the steep expenses of recruiting a replacement, of training a successor, of slower technology advancement in the interim while there is a vacant position. Such transitions could easily cost $100,000 each. Further, recruiting an equivalent engineer to a company not offering health care would be a challenge. The same can be said of other skilled positions, from press operator to programmer to executive.

As for losing positive leverage over the health of the workforce, companies in the vanguard of containing health costs do it by managing health. In the process, they enjoy improved productivity, higher morale, less absenteeism, and lower workers' compensation charges.

Companies in the vanguard of containing health costs do it by managing health. In the process, they are enjoying improved productivity, higher morale, less absenteeism, and lower workers' compensation charges.

Where health plans are well designed, including such amenities as on-site primary care, employees see their employer as making an investment in their families. That commitment creates a long-term bond. It acts much like tuition reimbursement and is appreciated by employees as a similar investment in their futures.

In contrast, dropping health care and telling people to go to the public exchanges for individual policies will inevitably be viewed as a step backward in a company's commitment to its workers. That will be true even if the employer gives the employees a raise or a "defined contribution" to help purchase the individual policies.

It will be especially true if the premiums for individual policies sold on private or public exchanges show a big hike over today's prices. Because of expensive ACA mandates on what a health insurance policy has to look like, some major insurers have decided not to offer policies in some states. That means less competition for individual policies, and less competition always means higher prices.

HARD COSTS

There is also a numbers side, the hard costs, in a company's go or no-go analysis.

Suppose an employer currently delivers health care at a total cost of about $8,500 per employee, which is tax deductible to the employer and tax exempt to the employee. If it drops the benefit, it would have to give an employee a taxable raise of more than $14,000 to buy an equivalent policy on an exchange. Plus, the employer may have to pay the $2,000 penalty for dropping coverage. The employee then comes out whole, but the company would be at least $7,500 worse off per employee than if it kept its health care benefit.

Suppose, instead, that a company wanted to drop coverage but be cost-neutral with its current expense of $8,500 per employee. In that scenario, it would limit the raise it gives to an employee to buy a policy to only $5,700.

Unfortunately, in most cases, that added compensation of $5,700 would not be enough to buy an equivalent policy on the exchange. That's true for many employees even if the employee qualifies for the subsidies offered by the federal government for buying a policy through a public exchange.

Here's a worse scenario for employees. If the employer drops coverage and offers no contribution, the worker gets hit hard. The employer may pay the $2,000 penalty, versus its previous $8,500 expense, so it saves a lot of money. But the employee is on the hook for a policy that currently could cost the national average of $16,000 or more for family coverage. That's before the rate increases that the new law could cause in the years ahead.

Analysts say a family premium could rise to $23,000 by 2020. That would be unbearable for an uncovered worker, even taking into account offsetting federal subsidies. And it gets close to the Cadillac tax on premiums of more than $27,500 in 2018.

At present premium prices, ACA's federal subsidies for a family of four range from about $3,000 for a household making $94,000 to $11,000 for a household making $31,000. Clearly, that's just not enough. The gap between the premiums and the subsidies could be huge. It's a good bet that future administrations will have to hike the subsidies, which carry an estimated price tag of $23 billion in 2014. That tab will escalate beyond 2014.

When Serigraph did its go or no-go exercise, the after-tax costs were about a wash for keeping or dropping coverage. That assumed a $5,000 annual contribution to each employee if we dropped coverage.

Taking into account the soft and hard costs, the best answer for many employers will be to continue to offer health care. The obvious exception among medium and large employers is those that do not value a long-term relationship with their workers. Where wages are low and turnover is high, in sectors such as restaurants, hotels, nursing homes, and call centers, employers may choose to pay the penalties. Those uncovered workers will have to head to the exchanges for individual policies and the subsidies.

THE INNOVATIONS IN HEALTH CARE ARE AT HAND

Serigraph's decision to stay in the health care game was made possible because managers in the private sector have invented a new business model that makes it tolerably affordable for companies to offer a health care benefit.

The maelstrom surrounding ObamaCare, which is insurance reform, not health care reform, has proved a monumental distraction from the fundamental problem facing the country—the staggering costs. What I call "real reform" of the delivery system has gained momentum at the grassroots level, as companies have become smarter managers of the supply chain for health care.

ObamaCare... is insurance reform,
not health care reform.

As three million companies make the go or no-go call on providing coverage, they need to take into account more than just the penalties imposed by the new federal law for bailing out of coverage and the costs they currently see before them. They also need to be acutely aware of the many innovative efforts across the private sector that add up to a radical reengineering of the delivery of health care in America. The innovators have taught us that the costs of health care can be dramatically reduced as workforce health is significantly improved.

Smart employers are doing a better job of improving workforce health while controlling costs.

Note: A widespread default to individual insurance and government plans would sharply raise the national health care bill, because governments and insurance companies are slow movers when it comes to systemic changes. They are not good at managing costs. They are the wrong horses to ride for innovation.

The right horses are sharp corporate payers that are revamping the delivery of health care. They are bending the inflation curve. They and their consumer/employees are the game changers.

Their collective, transformative innovations add up to a megatrend. Their successes make this an optimistic book, regardless of the impact of ObamaCare on the health care insurance industry.

2

PRIVATE PAYERS FORGE
DISRUPTIVE NEW
BUSINESS MODEL

C HIEF EXECUTIVE OFFICERS across America, with a few exceptions, should offer a class-action apology for allowing the economics of health care to get totally out of whack.

By any financial measure, the existing business model for health care in the United States is busted, and the people in the corporate offices let it happen. They are paid lots of money to fix major problems facing their companies and the economy, and only a few have raised health care to the level of a strategic priority.

They didn't apply the golden rule—he who has the gold rules. They are the payers for about half of the national health care bill, and they didn't rule. (Indirectly, they pay for the other half of the nation's health care bill, the public half, as well, through the taxes paid by their companies and from the taxes taken out of the wages of their employees.) Specifically:

- The CEOs didn't create a marketplace to bring supply and demand disciplines to the delivery of care.
- They didn't engage their employees as active managers and consumers of medical treatments.
- They gave in on union contracts that enabled workers to practice economic misbehaviors.
- They didn't create a culture of health in their organizations.
- They allowed providers to vertically integrate the health care supply chain, to the great disadvantage of employers and their employees.
- They didn't deploy the managerial expertise of their teams to build a better business model for health care.

Fortunately, there is an amendment to the CEO apology. A growing vanguard of innovative CEOs has taken measure of the magnitude of the challenge and has moved to action. The CEOs' collective efforts have given birth to a disruptive business model that works. They are CEOs or former CEOs like Paul Purcell of Robert W. Baird & Co., Jim Hagedorn of Scotts Miracle-Gro, Steve Burd of Safeway, Tim Sullivan of Bucyrus International, and Bill Linton of Promega. (More on their stories later.)

A growing vanguard of innovative CEOs...has moved to action. The CEOs' collective efforts have given birth to a disruptive business model that works.

This book is full of innovations that executives across the country have implemented in their companies. But before we dive into the new model, let's look at why the current model just isn't working.

A MODEL IN NEED OF REPAIR

There is a plethora of ways that the current model is broken, tracing back to World War II, when employers added health care benefits as a way around wage controls. The evidence for the current breakdown includes:

- Costs have roughly doubled every eight years for the last four decades. At this rate, health benefits could equal base pay for many jobs within a decade. Some manufacturers report that the cost of insuring their workers exceeds that of production materials.

- Costs per employee for family coverage average $16,351 in the United States, according to the Kaiser Family Foundation, and exceed $20,000 in many organizations. Those are painfully high numbers for any employer.

- The Milliman Medical Index put 2013 costs at $22,030 per family of four, split 58 percent to the employer and 42 percent to employee in the combination of premiums, deductibles, and copays. The employee share of $9,144 exceeds the cost of food for most families.

- Prices for procedures vary wildly—as much as 300 to 400 percent within regions, even from hospital to hospital and clinic to clinic within the same health system. It is pricing chaos.

- More than 40 percent of U.S. companies don't offer health care insurance. The prime reason is escalating costs.

- Medical bills are now the leading cause of personal bankruptcy in the country.

- The U.S. government has been running trillion-dollar annual deficits, with health care entitlements a leading cause of the red ink. Major national priorities like education and environmental advances are being crowded out. A recent defense secretary said the Pentagon spends more on health care than on weapons.

- Many state budgets hemorrhage red ink or incur greater debt because of undermanaged health costs, especially in Medicaid.
- Some municipalities have gone bankrupt, with public employee health costs as a major contributor to their insolvency.

Spending on Health Care as a Percentage of Gross Domestic Product, 1960 to 2005

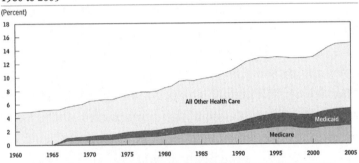

Source: Congressional Budget Office based on data on spending on health services and supplies, as defined in the national health expenditure accounts, maintained by the Centers for Medicare and Medicaid Services.

Note: Amounts for Medicare are gross federal spending on the program. Amounts for Medicaid include spending by the federal government and the states.

Projected Spending on Health Care as a Percentage of Gross Domestic Product

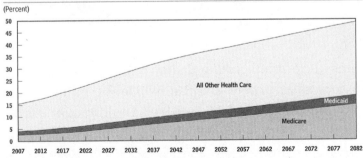

Source: Congressional Budget Office.

Note: Amounts for Medicare are net of beneficiaries' premiums. Amounts for Medicaid are federal spending only.

A recent defense secretary said the Pentagon spends more on health care than on weapons.

This catalog of negative consequences adds up to a complete indictment of the existing business model for medicine, even as doctors and their teams deliver minor miracles on a daily basis on the treatment side. U.S. physicians and nurses are on the cutting edge when people get sick. Almost all practitioners deliver empathetic, professional, caring service.

But fixing sick people isn't good enough if it bankrupts or financially stresses them, their companies, and governments in the process. The economic side of medicine has to be as effective as the medical side.

The Hippocratic Oath for physicians—"First, Do No Harm"—has to extend beyond medical outcomes to the economics of care.

WHO'S GOING TO FIX IT?

Unrelenting health care inflation has generated extreme frustration at private companies. Unlike public sector business managers, they cannot pass along cost escalation. Their customers won't allow them to pass along excess costs. With nowhere to turn for relief, private sector payers are revolting. They have learned that management has been the missing link in U.S. health care, that management disciplines have to be brought to bear.

Put on another hat. Think about what a turnaround manager would do if confronted with a totally busted business model, one that has been going the wrong way for decades? The turnaround guru would look at the existing players—insurance companies, provider organizations, policy wonks, health care academics, and political experts in health care—and that manager would be highly skeptical of their ability to turn things around. That manager would conclude that the major players in health care have been talking reform for decades but have demonstrated little success.

Major players in health care have been talking reform for decades but have demonstrated little success.

Our expert would be looking for a clean sheet of paper. Our turnaround tough guy would look for a new business model.

Some hospital initiatives have slowed the cost escalation, especially among providers that have employed the lean disciplines that were introduced into manufacturing with great success 40 years ago. But only about 1 percent of providers, like the Cleveland Clinic and Gundersen Health and ThedaCare in Wisconsin, have adopted transformational lean methods.

Provider corporations that own hospitals and clinics, whether for-profit or not-for-profit, have had little incentive to fix the old system heretofore. These huge organizations have profited handsomely in the current dysfunctional environment. While they face government price controls, they face neither market disciplines nor regulatory price controls on their private sector book of business. They see limited competition. This means there is little incentive to cut costs. They are almost immovable objects. Why should they move? Life, for them, is good.

Provider corporations... have profited handsomely in the current dysfunctional environment.

It is also good for health insurers.

Since the main assets of health insurance companies are their networks of providers and the volume discounts they bargain for, it's unrealistic to expect them to be agents for reform. Why would they push their de facto partners hard when they need them and when they get a cut of the rising costs? Indeed, they have a huge *disincentive* to drive down overall costs and premium prices, since doing so would reduce their revenue increases.

The Affordable Care Act may expand health care coverage to 94 percent of Americans, but it makes the cost outlook worse. Under "medical loss ratio" rules, health insurers may keep for themselves no more than 15 percent of large company plan premiums and no more than 20 percent of small company premiums. This gives them every reason to want the other 85 percent or 80 percent—the amount they're obliged to spend on medical care and quality improvement—to be as high as possible so their 15 percent to 20 percent cut in dollars is protected.

It's not that health insurance companies aren't seeking some efficiencies, but their intrinsic motivations for reform are not compelling. Cost reduction is just not where they live day in and day out.

Would-be reformers who assume that competition among insurance companies will rectify the economic ills of medicine in America are simply misguided. Competition among third-party payers has existed for decades, with little resulting reform. Why would that change going forward?

The real horse to ride for reform has to be the payers—employers and their employees as consumers. Because of the economic pain surrounding health care, the reform campaign has been building in the private sector, where most innovation takes place.

Private payers are saying, "Enough already!" It's time to take charge.

They are the parties demanding what I call real health care reform. For decades they have faced stiff premium increases, year in and year out. A 10 percent increase on a low base cost in the old days was bad enough, but a 10 percent increase on premiums on a higher base, as high as $20,000 per employee, is untenable.

There are two major ironies in all this. First, the high costs caused the access issue that ObamaCare tries to address. If costs were low, access wouldn't be an issue. Second, because of decades of hyperinflation of health costs, because costs are so bloated, huge savings await companies that manage health care costs aggressively.

ENTERING THE GAME: WHAT BUSINESSES ARE DOING NOW

The long-AWOL executives of corporations have come belatedly, but decisively, to the challenge of managing the chaos on the economic side of American health care. No other vendor would get away with double-digit increases for decades.

CEOs, CFOs, and COOs in front-running companies are doing radical surgery on an unsustainable system. They are bringing management concepts and marketplace principles to bear. They are tackling what they see as an undermanaged supply chain.

That means:

- Elevating their employees from passive, entitled recipients to engaged consumers
- Insisting on transparent prices and quality

- Creating incentives and disincentives and a culture of smart consumerism
- Moving business to the highest-value providers.
- Treating health care vendors with respect, but demanding performance
- Creating a culture of fitness and health at their companies
- Making workforce health and health costs a strategic priority

In the process of making health care a top-of-mind issue, they are inventing a far better business model for the delivery of health care for the whole nation. In that sense, it is patriotic work.

Before they got fully engaged, it was common practice for managers to use the one-time tactic of shifting costs to employees. But there is only so much mileage there. Employees can only afford so much for care, especially since wage increases have generally been anemic for more than a decade.

The executives have learned that health costs can be managed, and they have discovered they are in the business of behavior change. They have calculated that a well-managed health plan can be a competitive advantage.

Consider the fundamental health care dynamics today: insurance companies have a *short-term*, transaction-based, impersonal relationship with the insured's employees.

The same *short-term* mentality is true of large corporations that run hospitals and clinics; they excel at reacting to, not preventing, medical problems. In the existing model, primary care office visits last six to eight minutes. Frontline doctors oversee 2,500 to 3,000 patients each, forcing them to act only as gatekeepers to more expensive and profitable specialists. They are paid by volumes of procedures. Theirs is a production-centered business model, not a patient-centered model.

In stark contrast, most, though not all, employers foster a mutually beneficial, *long-term* relationship with their employees. Assuming a career of 25 to 40 years and an average of $16,000 in annual health costs per employee, the mutual bill for health care over a long career can easily exceed a half million dollars.

Conclusion? Employers and employees are the only health care players with a deep mutual interest in a *long-term* game plan. They are in a health care compact for many years.

Employers and employees are the only health care players with a deep mutual interest in a long-term game plan.

Good health profits them both—not just in workplace productivity and happiness but also in their respective budgets. Remember: the average split in the country on health care expenses for a family plan is 72 percent employer and 28 percent employee. (Some experts put the employee share higher.)

What better team for fixing the broken business model than employers and employees? This is the tandem of payers to ride for real reform. And that is exactly what's happening.

THE STEPS COMPANIES ARE TAKING

Exasperated private payers, led by large and medium employers, are staging a revolt. Defenseless small companies, who face the stiffest premium increases year in and year out, are joining the march. Companies with workforces as small as ten people are racing toward self-insurance as a first step, thereby assuming the risks, responsibilities, and rewards of keeping costs in check.

Their second step has been to roll out consumer-driven plans that engage employees in becoming responsible users and buyers of medical services.

That, in turn, requires data sleuths, known as transparency and analytics vendors, who collect and slice and dice the medical charges and outcomes from many health care transactions to shine a light on prices and quality. They offer clear comparisons of costs and quality. It is a new lens that allows consumers to make sound decisions on where to get care.

The payers' fourth step is to contract for rigorous on-site providers to manage health. Their health teams tackle chronic diseases, believed to cause 80 percent of health costs.

---

*Chronic diseases [are] believed to cause
80 percent of health costs.*

The sum of these kinds of structural changes in health care delivery constitutes a better model, a disruptive model. They spell real reform. And they create a virtuous linkage of improved workforce health and lower costs.

REFORM TAKES A VILLAGE

Bending the cost curve doesn't come easy. It takes effective management. It requires culture change. It means difficult behavior change at the personal and organizational level. It entails business risks. But as innovative corporations are proving, it can be accomplished.

Major change doesn't happen in a corporation without leadership from the C-suite, from the CEO on down through the management team. And it requires engaging the troops. It is simultaneously a top-down and bottom-up revolution. That sounds paradoxical, but it decidedly is not. The success of any major corporate initiative depends on that vital interaction.

Relying on human resource managers and benefit specialists to manage something as large and strategic as workforce health just doesn't work. People who choose that profession tend to be caregivers, not change agents.

The reason the revolt is accelerating is that the top managers have come to two realizations: health costs could take their enterprises down and they can be managed. They have learned they can turn a negative to a positive.

Joel Quadracci, CEO of Quad/Graphics, the nation's second-largest printer, said publicly, "Who would have thought that health care would become a competitive advantage for a printing company?"

Or, I might add, for many other companies?

The stakes are high.

For instance, one company (Robert W. Baird & Co., see box on following page) expects to cut at least 10 percent from its annual billion-dollar health care coverage bill via best practices. At seven times cash flow, that would mean an addition to that company's enterprise value of $700 million.

BEST BUSINESS PRACTICES
IN HEALTH CARE

We can learn from what these innovative companies are doing. This book will lay out the three-year playbook to move from a broken business model to best practices for health care delivery—to a reinvented, disruptive model. It will tell stories of private companies that are leading the way in proving that costs can be curbed, even flatlined.

They are not talking reform. They're doing it. Their CEOs are leading the charge.

ONE COMPANY'S PRAGMATIC JOURNEY

Robert W. Baird & Co., an employee-owned financial services company, has taken a long, pragmatic road to better health care results.

CEO Paul Purcell made it a strategic issue a decade ago, starting with a wellness program at its Milwaukee headquarters in 2004. The self-insured company, which has 2,700 workers, offered $100 to each worker and another $100 to each worker's spouse for undergoing an online health risk assessment about eating and lifestyle habits. It also offered biometric screening for cholesterol, blood pressure, and glucose levels.

"We were experiencing 15 percent to 20 percent increases in health costs at the time," explained company benefits manager Lisa Mrozinski in an interview. "We had to get that under control."

That initial effort to turn things around was underwhelming. "We had a 45 percent participation rate," Mrozinski said. For many workers, $100 wasn't enough to overcome their distrust of the company's health insurance administrator, who oversaw the program. "We could have reassured them 100 times that HIPAA (federal privacy law) assured their privacy, but there was still that lack of trust."

In 2005, Baird hired an outside vendor and spent that year educating its staff on the value of preventive care. "You may think you're really healthy, but until you go through the process we can provide, you may not be aware that you're pre-diabetic or have high cholesterol," she said. "The idea is, know your numbers."

In 2006, Baird made it expensive to skip the annual health evaluation—a $50 monthly surcharge per worker. In 2007, the company enacted a $50 monthly surcharge for covered spouses who didn't participate. Participation shot to 96 percent in 2006 and 98 percent in 2007.

Baird also launched an online transparency tool that allowed workers to compare provider prices for certain medical tests and procedures in the area.

Health care increases dropped to the 8 percent to 10 percent range.

Meanwhile, the company tried and scrapped two more ideas that didn't work: health coach calls to everyone to discuss their test results and a $100 reward for taking online health courses or working with a health coach. "People didn't like the health coach calling them," Mrozinski said, "and few people were interested in getting the $100."

In 2008, Baird offered a high-deductible alternative to its regular health insurance program. In 2009, it made the high-deductible plan mandatory, but created a health savings contribution of $250 for single workers and $500 for a couple or family.

"Our costs leveled off—2 percent to 5 percent—in 2010 through 2012," she said. The company shared some of the savings with associates through higher contributions to their accounts to $450 (single) and $900 (couple or family) in 2011 and 2012.

Through all these changes, the company still pays 75 percent of premiums.

More change is underway. In 2012, Baird required its employees to pass three of five risk-factor tests—cholesterol, blood pressure, glucose level, tobacco use, and body mass index—or work with a coach and take an online health class. Those who wouldn't cooperate—about 2 percent—had to pay a $50 to $100 monthly surcharge and forfeited the company's contribution to their Health Savings Account.

Purcell said the program might seem intrusive, but he believes it is strategic and necessary.

3

THREE-YEAR GAME PLAN CAN FLATLINE COMPANY HEALTH COSTS

DOUG VANDENBERG, a director for Thomas H. Lee Partners (THL), a private equity company, sees a major competitive advantage in getting health costs under control in its portfolio companies. He knows he can't wave a magic wand and get there in a quarter or two, but the payoffs are so great that he wants to get there as soon as possible. He has asked the executives of the 18 THL companies to move to a full set of best practices in an urgent time frame. Some of those companies are close to a full new business model for delivery of health care; some newer companies in the portfolio are just getting started.

It should come as no surprise that the companies farthest down the road to best practices deliver a full health benefit at one-third less than those who operate with poorly designed plans.

If he can get all his portfolio companies up to speed, he can knock 10 to 20 percent off the combined billion-dollar tab for employer and employees. At 10 percent savings, THL saves $100 million. At seven times cash flow, THL would add $700 million to its market value. That's real money any way you cut it.

Vandenberg described his company's journey this way:

> In our role as private equity investor at Thomas H. Lee Partners, we have a keen role in ensuring our companies grow quickly and operate as efficiently as possible. As with the economy in general, more and more of our portfolio companies are service businesses where labor is the largest cost component, and health care expense is not far behind. With continual growth well beyond inflation, this domain demanded our attention.
>
> Traditionally, most people believe that health care costs are simply an immovable fact of life. Every year a certain percentage of people will experience accidents or become sick, go to the doctor and then dutifully follow the doctor's orders. Along the way they will accumulate bills to then be divided between patient/employee and employer. Too often the employee thinks this expense is borne by the insurance company named on their insurance card

and doesn't realize this expense ultimately flows right back to their employer and them.

With a broad portfolio of businesses, we were able to use this group to learn from their experiences—good, bad, or otherwise—to identify best practices. In digging deeply into the problems and different experiences, a key lesson was that medical expenses and consumption are not immovable monuments, but actually are subject to many opportunities for reduction and management.

Three sources of opportunity arose: 1) One-third of medical spend is waste due to unnecessary or duplicative services; 2) Three-quarters of medical spend is due to preventable, lifestyle-related diseases, and 3) Not all providers are equal in terms of quality and cost. While we certainly can't solve or eliminate these three issues, they represented ripe opportunities. Not only could we reduce health care expense but we could do so by improving the health and lives of our employees.

How do you get there? By putting in place the right structure and incentives for the decision maker: the patient or the employee. The current system is unique in that the individual making the purchase decision is usually divorced from the costs and often not enabled to make optimal decisions. In short, employees need to be given better motivation and information. The motivation comes in the form of consumer-directed health plan designs and incentives for things outside the scope of plan design, such as tobacco-free premium discounts.

The information comes in the form of transparency tools and best-in-class care coordination. Proper care coordination enables you to spend more on additional services for the few who drive most of the costs in any year, yet come out ahead once the savings from medical cost avoidance are factored in.

At our firm, we observed these best practices empirically in our investment portfolio and then codified them into recommendations that have been implemented. They are now delivering fantastic results. Reducing health care costs frees up cash that can instead be reinvested in the business to fuel growth.

Helping employees improve their health is right for the company's bottom line and is doing right by our employees. Healthier employees are happier, demonstrate less absenteeism and presenteeism, and are more productive. This is a win for everyone involved.

As with THL, there are a lot of moving parts in the disruptive new business model that is taking shape in the private sector across the country, and they all have to work in concert to get the best results. Think of it like a high-quality car that is fast, efficient, and affordable. It has a number of platforms: power, drivetrain, chassis, wheels and steering system, and electronic controls. Under each platform are the components. They all have to be working in concert for the car to operate at a high level.

The typical company has adopted one or a few of the best practices, such as consumer incentives and disincentives, and they see some relief from the relentless inflation in health benefits. Many are still using the unworkable insurance model that features low deductibles and coinsurance.

To get to a deeper, more sustainable model, they all need a complete game plan that encompasses most of the innovations discovered by private payers in recent years.

Reengineered Health Care Management Model

Health as Asset
- Individual Health Plans
- Education/Communication
- Health Report Cards
- Wellness Programs

Self-Insurance
- Stop-Loss Coverage
- Large Case Management
- Network Selection

Consumer-Driven Plan
- HRA or HSA
- High Deductible

Health Care Analytics
- Financial Dashboard
- Health Dashboard
- Savings Targets

Engaged Employee/ Employer

Transparency on Value
- Price Ranges
- Quality Ratings

Disease Management
- Six Sigma Rigor
- Free Prevention
- Health Risk Assessments
- Health Coaching

Centers of Value
- Brokered Buys
- Bundled Prices
- Rebates for Good Choices
- Reference-Based Pricing

On-site Primary Care
- Holistic Care
- Proactive Care
- Utilization Management
- Supply Chain Control
- EAP
- Workers' Comp.

They need a playbook that gets them to a full set of best practices.

In later chapters we'll cover these ideas in depth, showing how various business leaders have intertwined best practices together into that playbook, but first, as an overview, let's look at the basics of the playbook.

START WITH SAVING MONEY THROUGH SELF-INSURANCE

So where does a company start in establishing a systemic model for the delivery of health care?

First, it does little good for a company to adopt innovative practices that save money if it is fully insured. The savings go to the pool of insured companies, of which it is only one member. The pool structure does spread the risks of expensive cases, but the insured company gets only a sliver of its own savings. You're married to stuck-in-the-mud companies.

Ergo, as Play One, private companies need to wean themselves off indemnity plans and move to self-insurance. Conventional wisdom has said that a corporation needs at least 500 employees to make the move to self-insurance, to create its own risk pool. But that advice is changing as smaller companies, desperate for savings on health care, get more aggressive. They are self-insuring with as few as 10 employees.

Private companies need to wean themselves off indemnity plans and move to self-insurance.

They offset the risk of getting hit with an expensive episode of care by buying stop-loss insurance to protect against catastrophic claims. Fortunately, there are now

44

a good number of insurers that are willing to offer catastrophic coverage at reasonable prices. (More on the gold rush to self-insurance in Chapter 4.)

INCENTIVIZE YOUR EMPLOYEES

Play Two in the playbook injects incentives and disincentives into the behaviors of employees.

Under old health plans with a $300 deductible and low coinsurance, there was little reason for an employee to be smart about health care decisions. Some of these "rich" plans still exist, mostly in the public sector. Once an employee blows through the deductible, a lion's share of the balance is paid by the company. It is mostly a free lunch for the employee.

But when the deductible is set at a higher amount—the median appears to be about $2,500—employee behaviors change on a dime. A Health Savings Account (HSA) or a Health Reimbursement Arrangement (HRA) usually offsets the high deductible, so the out-of-pocket expenses by an employee can stay about the same. But it's the employee's money in the accounts, and that makes all the difference.

Why would an employee spend $3,000 of his own money for an MRI when the same procedure can be purchased for $525? Why would he go to an emergency room for $600 for a routine medical issue when he could go to a clinic for $160? The answer is easy. Employees choose the less expensive options if they are in consumer-driven plans. They become responsible consumers. They save money for their company, they save money for their fellow employees who are in the same self-insured pool, and they save money for themselves.

But if they are not on the hook for payments in one way or another, they make wrong decisions all day, every day. Why not? They are rational economic beings, and it's not their money at stake.

The appropriate incentives and disincentives create a virtuous circle of savings. (More on the consumer-driven play in Chapter 5.)

IMPLEMENTATION OF PLAYS ONE AND TWO

Going self-insured and installing a consumer-driven plan is plenty to accomplish in the first year of a three-year march to best practices. Self-insurance takes some planning time because the company has to pick the best network of providers for its employees. The network can be acquired through a health plan, through a TPA—third-party administrator—or can be put together through a collaboration of employers. Claims processing can also be bought from multiple sources.

Companies often use a broker/consultant to help with those choices. There is some variation in the depth of the discounts negotiated from providers, so it pays to shop your business. But chasing discounts only makes a difference of a couple of percentage points.

The big deal is choosing a high-value network with lots of choice and the right geographic alignment. The consultant can also help in selecting the right level of stop-loss insurance at the best premium.

The first year has to be filled with a lot of communication with co-workers about your new consumer-driven plan. You are not just changing your plan design. You are committing to a lot of education about how to be a good consumer. You are aiming at engagement of your people with the strategic agenda of the company on health and health cost management. It's a culture change, and that's not easy.

You will need every form of communication available at the company. Group meetings are fine, but, in the end, one-on-one meetings with each employee will be needed. All that takes time.

You will need every form of communication available at the company. Group meetings are fine, but, in the end, one-on-one meetings with each employee will be needed.

With incentives in place, utilization will drop sharply from overutilization to sensible levels. But that's just the start on consumerism.

Intelligent Health Care Spending Happens through Transparency

Play Three needs to follow shortly behind the engagement of the employees as smart buyers of health care. It's the transparency piece.

You can't ask people to be intelligent consumers without giving them good information. They, of course, will want to know the prices of various procedures. At Serigraph, we have displayed price ranges at area hospitals and clinics for more than a hundred procedures on our intranet site. Many other companies are following suit in offering transparency.

But employees and spouses will also want to know about the quality ratings of the providers. That information has been hard to come by, but new players are moving to meet that demand in the emerging marketplace for health care. And Medicare is releasing more and more quality data, such as infection rates at the nation's hospitals. At Serigraph, we are now able to give health facilities an A, B, or C rating on quality. (We are not able to drill down to the doctor level for quality—yet.)

A number of entrepreneurial vendors have rushed to fill the market need for information on health care value. Companies are buying a transparency module for several dollars per month per employee. (More on the transparency play in Chapter 6.)

Promoting Centers of Value

The next step, Play Four in the playbook, is to promote Centers of Value. Don't you, as an employer/payer, have a moral obligation to search out the best providers of health care for quality, service, and price and then make them known and available for your people? Is it ethical or smart to set up a network that includes sub-par health care vendors? Further, health care bills for elective procedures can be sharply reduced at the highest-value centers. It may require some travel time to get to those centers, but it's worth it.

Indeed the savings can be so great that companies are now offering rewards or rebates to employees who make the trip to the Centers of Value.

Those centers deserve our business. They have earned the added volume by being good at what they do. Further, the more volume they win, the more proficient they become and the more they can spread their overheads to make their prices even lower and more competitive. It's a virtuous circle.

That set of dynamics is called a marketplace. Together, CEOs and employees can move their business and make a market happen. (More on Centers of Value in Chapter 7.)

TIMETABLE FOR PLAYS THREE, FOUR, AND FIVE

The introduction of Plays Three and Four can be accomplished in year two. Again, there are vendors in the developing marketplace that can help you get there.

Play Five can be easily added in year two, as well. It is the leap past the Byzantine pricing system that has been put into place since the government got heavily into the business of being a health care payer.

PRICE IN BUNDLES

The use of complex, government-engendered pricing codes, procedure by procedure, is a mess that should be dumped by private payers. It is a pricing morass that promotes production medicine, where volumes of procedures trump value. Pay by procedure and what do you get? Lots of procedures.

Pay by procedure and what do you get?
Lots of procedures.

In days long gone, manufacturers used "piece rates" to pay factory workers. They rewarded volume. It never worked very well, because high production was marred by high scrap rates. It was a good 40 years ago that most manufacturers dropped production-based pay schemes. Yet, health care still operates that way.

One answer for companies is to seek out what are known as "bundled prices." That means a single bill for everything involved in an episode of care. Serigraph, for instance, buys knee replacements for as low as $27,500. That's all-in. There are no extra bills for anesthesia, drugs, recovery room—or anything else. It is the ultimate in transparency.

If some providers can do it, they all can. Private payers are demanding bundled prices for surgeries, imaging, colonoscopies, and other preventive services, and they are getting them. There are brokers out there who can help with such pricing arrangements.

In addition, payers are starting to pay annual retainers for services like primary care—one bill for a year of care. (More about these disruptive pricing models in Chapter 8.)

ON-SITE HEALTH CLINICS

As a company enters the third year of building its new model for care, the potential savings get even better. It's time to take back primary care from the big hospital corporations. Play Six can be done with an on-site primary care clinic.

It can be a full-time clinic if the company is big enough. Or, for mid-size employers, it can be a part-time clinic, with the hours determined by the needs of employees.

Even though it hasn't happened broadly yet, some smaller companies teamed up in joint clinics.

These clinics usually include nurse practitioners, physician assistants, nurses, and health coaches. Large clinics offer full-time primary care doctors, while smaller clinics can contract for part-time doctors, dieticians, and chiropractors. A few offer acupuncturists and behavioral health experts.

It is not hard to establish on-site care, because there is a stampede of new provider organizations that offer these services to private corporations. The savings from taking back the front end of the supply chain for health care are immediate and enormous.

Instead of being victims of abuse on the economic side of medicine in the United States, the payers are back in charge, as they should be. The golden rule is back at work. (More on proactive, on-site primary care in Chapter 9.)

MANAGE EMPLOYEE HEALTH

Play Seven flows from Play Six. With an on-site health team offering intimate, holistic care to members, rigorous face-to-face management of chronic diseases can be launched and attained. It can't be done with brochures, websites, and sermons on health. We're talking Six Sigma management that tolerates no defects in the process of dealing with chronic diseases like diabetes, hypertension, asthma, and depression.

CEOs, for instance, can demand that all diabetics in their firms be brought under control for the three relevant drug tests. That would mean 100 percent of the diabetics in their workforce have the disease under control as measured by three blood tests, compared to about one-third nationally.

There is big money to be saved, because it is generally accepted that some 80 percent of U.S. health costs derive from chronic conditions. (More on this in Chapter 10.)

REGARD HEALTH AS AN ASSET

Finally, as all the platforms and moving parts of the new business model for health care are put into place in a company, a whole new outlook develops. Play Eight is to treat health as an asset—a personal asset, a corporate asset, and a financial asset.

Healthy employees are much better off financially than their unhealthy peers. And healthy, financially stable employees are more productive than employees with health problems. Think about it: A healthy workforce is a huge competitive advantage. Good health is a blessing in so many ways. (More on health as a financial asset in Chapter 11.)

The three-year march to best practices in health care management is the beginning of an unending journey to the mountaintop of best care practices. But it is a beginning that has to be made if companies are going to continue to offer health care as a benefit without destroying their bottom lines.

Three-Year Road Map to Best Practices in Delivery of Health Care

Year One
Getting Started

1. Go Self-Insured.

2. Introduce Consumer-Driven Health Plan.

3. Set up tiered drug management to promote generics.

4. Change culture to health care vs. sick care.

Year Two
Buying Smart

1. Make prices, quality transparent.

2. Seek out Centers of Value.

3. Demand bundled bills.

Year Three
Proactive Care

1. Install on-site primary care.

2. Create medical home.

3. Tackle chronic diseases with Six Sigma disciplines.

4. Treat health as financial asset.

MORE INNOVATIONS
IN THE WORK EVERY DAY

Beyond the three-year game plan, new innovations are constantly arriving on the front lines in the battle to control costs and improve health care delivery. That is the beauty of a marketplace where continual innovation is a requirement for survival.

Corporate stewards can graft the stream of innovations onto their new business model as they justify themselves in terms of savings and health improvements. It's all about leadership and management—aggressive, innovative, pragmatic, proactive management.

That has been the missing link in American health care. But no more. Managers in the private sector are stepping up. They are moving rapidly to a game plan and playbook that has been tested and proven at the grassroots level.

4

SELF-INSURANCE: COMPANIES KEEP THEIR HEALTH SAVINGS

A CROSS THE COUNTRY, there is a groundswell of companies moving from insurance plans to self-insurance. This is because aggressive executives don't want to be lumped into an insured pool of passive payers who are doing little to control their health care costs. Why would they want to share costs and risks in a pool that includes companies that are paying more than $20,000 a year per family when they have learned that if they manage intelligently they can provide the same health benefit for $10,000 or less per year? Why would they want to share risks with companies where the diabetics are largely out of control when they have learned that they can help almost all of their diabetics get under control?

For a company with 500 employees, that's a differential of $5 million per year. It's the monetized value of the gap between worst and best practices in health cost management. Best-practice management constitutes a significant competitive advantage. For some companies, those savings are a matter of survival.

Large employers with more than 1,000 employees are leading the charge to self-insurance. Nearly nine out of 10 now take on most of their own health care risk, compared to just over half in 1998. That means that almost six out of 10 employees in the private sector are covered in self-insurance plans, according to Employer Benefit Research Institute (EBRI).

Small- and mid-size companies have been slower to move, but brokers report that they are starting to move in the same direction.

EBRI reported that Massachusetts saw an increase in self-insurance among all sizes of companies after that state adopted health care reform similar to ObamaCare. So expect the trend to accelerate.

Benefits of Self-Insurance under ACA

For openers, going to a self-insured plan gives a company an exemption from the ACA tax of several points on insured plans. Other advantages include an escape from ACA and state mandates, from state insurance taxes, and from insurance company overhead charges.

A decade ago, it was conventional wisdom that companies had to employ at least 500 employees to take on the risk of self-insurance. Today, companies with as few as 10 employees are taking that route. They want to keep offering a health care benefit, but they can't afford the double-digit annual premium increases levied by fully insured plans.

Executives in small- and medium-size firms have watched innovators like Quad/Graphics, Safeway, and Briggs & Stratton use their management skills to reduce health costs by as much as one-third below the national average. One-third! Naturally, the smaller companies want those savings, too. And they can't get them if they are in an insurance pool with companies that don't manage costs.

STOP-LOSS INSURANCE

The enabler for smaller companies is to shop for what's called stop-loss insurance at the right level to protect themselves against catastrophic medical incidents or a rash of claims. Take, for example, a baby born prematurely. The medical bill for caring for the baby can easily be a half million to a million dollars. Larger companies can absorb catastrophic risks, but small and medium companies can't.

The good news is that stop-loss protection is readily available. At Serigraph, we buy catastrophic coverage at

$200,000. We stop our losses at $200,000 and pay a premium of $250,000 per year to do so.

In a good year for health, we never have a case that hits that level. In a bad year, we may have several cases for which the losses exceed $200,000. In good years, the insurance companies make out; in the bad years, they absorb the overages.

To accommodate the desires of smaller companies to control their own destiny in health care benefits, UnitedHealthcare has reduced its minimum from 100 employees in a firm to 10. Other health insurers go down to 25-employee groups.

In an unexpected twist, some small employers with healthy workforces will use ObamaCare to their advantage: they will move to self-insurance to save money. Then, if they have a bad year with a couple losses that exceed their stop-loss limit, and they are faced with premium hikes for the following year's stop-loss coverage, they can bail out to the new health insurance exchanges. They won't be penalized there, because ObamaCare requires guaranteed issue, which means pooled premiums that cover costly pre-existing conditions.

In an unexpected twist, some small employers with healthy workforces will use ObamaCare to their advantage: they will move to self-insurance to save money.

In effect, the small companies have a backup plan mandated by the federal government. They have a safe harbor if self-insurance doesn't work out.

The converse is also true. Companies with unhealthy, often older, workforces will default to the insured policies to get the guaranteed issue. That, of course, means higher premiums for all the firms in those insured pools.

There is a win-win dynamic in the emerging business model for the delivery of health care. As self-insured employers do a better and better job of managing health, they cut down the number of high-risk employees in their workforces. Fewer diabetics out of control is just one example.

Those better management practices spell fewer medical catastrophes. Indeed, the metrics at best-practice companies show sharp drops in hospital admissions.

Over time, fewer catastrophes should spell lower premiums for stop-loss insurance. It should be a virtuous loop.

For companies with fewer than 50 employees, the median stop-loss (or deductible) was $35,000 in 2012. For firms with 51 to 100 employees, it was $45,000. For all companies, the average was $80,000.

Brokers can be very helpful in shopping for a reinsurer that provides stop-loss coverage. And they can help executives decide on the right level of risk for their companies.

The level will vary as a function of the company's size, financial status and outlook, and with its appetite for risk.

Administering Claims

Companies that self-insure still need a health plan that offers a network of providers and discounts. And they need an Administrative Services Organization (ASO) to administer claims. Almost no company wants to process its own claims.

Fortunately, the big health insurers like the ASO business, so they offer not only the stop-loss insurance but also the discounts obtained from their network of providers and their transaction services. They like group contracts far more than individual policies for health insurance.

Most small- and some mid-size companies also cover themselves for "aggregate" losses to protect themselves against a bad year overall for medical losses. The most common policy is to protect at more than 125 percent of expected claims for a given year. Larger companies, however, which spread the risks over their larger pool of self-insured lives, often skip the aggregate policy premium.

THE MAIN DEAL is to get your company self-insured. But self-insurance is just a launch pad for other reforms. By itself, it doesn't yield big savings.

Once self-insured, a company can embark on other reforms, such as installing consumer-driven incentives, making prices and quality of procedures transparent, purchasing from Centers of Value, aggressively managing chronic diseases, and offering proactive primary care.

The door is unlocked to real reform and the major savings that come with the more effective business model.

LESSONS LEARNED
on Self-Insured Plans

☑ Join the trend to self-insurance to control your health care destiny.

☑ Small employers can now go self-insured, too.

☑ Ask your broker about the right level of stop-loss coverage.

☑ Self-insurance alone does not get the job done; it is one in a set of management tools.

5

CONSUMER-DRIVEN:
COMPANIES ENGAGE EMPLOYEES

I T WAS A TOUGH CALL for GE. Its health care group sells lots of highly profitable imaging equipment to hospitals, but it needed to get its $2.5 billion health care bill under control. Its executives, from CEO Jeff Immelt on down, wanted to implement a consumer-driven health plan (CDHP). But they knew full well that such plans cut utilization, including rampant overutilization of imaging tests on its MRI and CT scanners. They knew their new CDHP would cut into the top lines of their good customers.

CDHPs combine a high deductible with an offsetting health account, which turns employees from passive recipients into responsible purchasers of health care. Employees become real consumers, and a company's health costs are reduced by 20 percent to 30 percent. That's big money. It takes a few years to get the behavior changes for the full savings, but a tourniquet on overutilization of procedures and tests takes hold immediately. Such plans have to be one of the first plays in a manager's game plan to bring a semblance of order to the chaos on the economic side of health care.

So GE bit the bullet in 2012 after an intense internal debate. *The Wall Street Journal* reported that the conglomerate dropped its low deductible plans and installed three plans for its half-million employees, dependents, and retirees, with deductibles ranging from $800 to $4,000.

As expected, costs dropped sharply, including a reduction in imaging tests on its own machines by more than 20 percent. Those decreases, of course, resulted in a revenue decrease to its customers, the hospital corporations.

THE GROWING CDHP TREND

A decade ago, the move to a consumer-driven health plan by a company was a significant business risk. Congress had just enabled Health Savings Accounts (HSAs) in 2002, but no corporate manager really knew if putting money into such employee incentives would drive better health behaviors. They didn't know if they could cut costs enough to get a return on the investment in the incentive program. Now we know.

Ten years of experience with high-deductible plans has removed the risk, and corporate managers are racing toward plans that put consumers in charge. This revolution to consumer-driven care is led by big payers who understand such cost savings and cash flows, such as Chrysler and JPMorgan Chase. UnitedHealthcare, the largest U.S. health plan, for example, offers its employees no other choice than a consumer-driven plan. Nearly 60 percent of large employers, including health insurers and health providers, offer CDHPs for their own legions of employees, and in 2012, a fifth of small employers (companies with 499 or fewer workers) offered a CDHP option. Indeed, with 16 percent of all covered employees now in consumer-driven plans, it can be argued that the nation is on the cusp of a consumer revolution.

Projections show that in five years, 40 percent of all employers will offer consumer plans. Further, expect CDHPs to become virtually the only plan offered by many employers by the end of the decade.

Cigna Corp., a health insurer, has been tracking the CDHP stampede closely. It sees nothing but an acceleration of the trend.

Cigna spokesman Joseph Mondy said, "As people become more familiar with CDHPs, you'll see migration. Why? Because they work. CDHPs will cost you less as an employee and as an employer, but you'll also see improvements in health outcomes. We have seven years of data to support that."

"CDHPs will cost you less as an employee and as an employer, but you'll also see improvements in health outcomes. We have seven years of data to support that."—JOSEPH MONDY, CIGNA CORP.

HEALTH CARE IS NOT AN OPEN BAR

This is not brain surgery. When people spend their own money, even if an employer gives it to them, they consume much more wisely than if someone else pays. Overconsumption is inevitable at free lunches or happy hours. The first question people ask at a wedding reception is: "Is this an open bar?"

If an employee has a $2,500 deductible and $1,500 in a Health Savings Account (HSA), which is about the average, and it's their money at stake, they start asking questions like, "How much is that knee replacement going to cost? And what's my share of the total cost?"

And they don't just look at price. Educated properly, they ask questions like: "What's the infection rate in your operating room?" Or, "How many knees do you do a year?" There is a direct correlation between volume and quality. Put another way, you don't want to go to a surgical team that only does a couple of operations per year; you want one that does a couple hundred.

Incentives alone don't create a consumer mentality in a company, but they surely help. If incentives and disincentives aren't aligned with corporate goals, all kinds of funny behaviors result.

Any emergency room (ER) doctor or nurse will tell you about Medicaid patients who endlessly abuse the system. People for whom Medicaid is free are behaving rationally when they demand the full range of services. They get a sore throat, call 911, demand an ambulance ride to the ER, and then insist on immediate treatment. Why not? After all, it's free. In the process of accessing an absurdly designed system, they abuse all three providers—911, the ambulance, and the professionals highly trained to deal with real triage. They are also abusing the taxpayer. Even more vexing, the entitlees even get pushy about their free medical "rights." They demand services, such as expensive tests.

Still more problematic, the Medicaid customers are generally regarded by hospitals as the most litigious. They look for excuses to sue.

When people spend their own money, even if it is given to them, they consume much more wisely than if someone else pays.

In the arena of health care and health costs, corporate managers have learned that they are in the business of changing such behaviors. Behavior change is never easy, but that's where the major savings lie.

Specifically, they are working with employees to improve these five behaviors:

- How employees utilize health care
- How they purchase care when they need it
- How they live their lives—their lifestyles
- How they follow regimens if they have a chronic disease condition
- How they collaborate with their doctor on long-term health

The immediate bang for the buck comes from reducing overutilization. For instance, instead of using a physical therapist for months of sessions after a surgery at $600 per hour, the employee-turned-consumer quickly figures out when to end the supervised treatments and do the exercises at home.

A person might tough out a sore throat and avoid an office visit that costs $160. If it gets worse, she would go to a convenience clinic or a doctor's office, but she wouldn't even think of going to an emergency room, where she'd pay $600 or more for a visit.

Employees have learned from media exposés that many surgeries on backs, joints, and hearts do little good. Many are unnecessary and cost a fortune. The smart consumer checks the studies and gets a second or third opinion before going under the knife.

Smart employers make those additional opinions free. There are companies that provide second opinions for a small fee. Smart employers also contract for relatively inexpensive advocates for their employees to help weigh tough decisions on surgery or no surgery.

The other behaviors are covered in other chapters to show how positive changes in all five are at the heart of the powerful new business model for health care.

CDHPs Increase Prevention Efforts

Critics of consumer-driven plans, usually from the political left-of-center, cite fears of underutilization because of high deductibles. But the studies show just the opposite.

If an employee is engaged in the economics of health care, in contrast to a patient with little or no skin in the game, he is more, not less, likely to utilize prevention and wellness programs. He quickly deduces that staying healthy not only can extend his life but can also save him and his company money.

There are many ways to elicit the help of employees in managing costs. On the front end, companies expose price and quality levels at all nearby hospitals and clinics. That enables workers to shop rigorously for the best value among various medical shops.

On the back end, smart employers offer incentives to plan members to audit medical bills for overcharges. Employees are allowed to keep up to half of any errors discovered, and they soon find that overcharges are rampant.

Engagement is the key. Old low-deductible, low-coinsurance plans put the plan member in a passive position, with little incentive to behave intelligently. They are disengaged recipients. The insurance company, the so-called third-party payer, pays the bills instead of the first party—the employee. Many theorists believe the third-party payer system is the root cause of America's high spending on health care. In the end, of course, it is the second party, the employer, who picks up most of the inflated bill.

Many theorists believe the third-party payer system is the root cause of America's high spending on health care.

HEALTH ACCOUNTS

A 2012 Employee Benefit Research Institute (EBRI) survey found 11.6 million accounts with either an HSA or Health Reimbursement Arrangement (HRA). That translates to almost 40 million covered people. (See HSA/HRA chart for differences.) The soaring popularity of HSAs and HRAs insulated them from major harm when ObamaCare was moving through Congress.

AN INSIDER STORY:
BUCYRUS INTERNATIONAL ADOPTS CDHP

When CEO Tim Sullivan led his unionized employees at Bucyrus International into a consumer-driven plan in 2008, the results were entirely consistent with other such conversions. The union steward told me that he was surprised that he had received no grievances after the $2,500 deductible and $2,500 savings accounts were voted on and installed. The steward said savings came in at 22 percent in year one. He wanted his steelworkers to share in some of the savings.

Sullivan had assured the union that if the steelworkers would follow him into the new health plan, he would expand operations in South Milwaukee, Wisconsin, where they build monster mining machines. Without the benefits savings, he told the employees that the plant would be uncompetitive in world markets. (Note: his executives and workers would be on the same plan. That's leadership.)

He followed through and invested $180 million in an expansion to keep up with demand for Bucyrus's tar sands shovels the size of a living room. The union gained members from new hires. It was a win-win-win for the company, the employees, and the union.

Bucyrus was one of the first major big unionized companies to make the leap to health accounts. Union leaders often make the illogical assumption that any requested changes in benefits are a step backward. They often equate high prices with better health care. But most managers and analysts have learned that there is no correlation between price and quality.

The good fortunes of Bucyrus in general resulted in a merger in 2011 with Caterpillar. Sullivan's shareholders reaped a big premium, and you can deduce that part of the high enterprise value had to come from its innovative management of benefits. The greater the cash flow, the higher the price.

COMPARE HSAs AND HRAs

Elements	Health Savings Accounts (HSAs)	Health Reimbursement Arrangements (HRAs)
Eligible Individuals/ Groups	Individuals, any size group. Must have HDHP coverage.	Any size group
Maximum Annual Contributions	Single HDHP coverage—$3,300 Family HDHP coverage—$6,550	Employer determined
Eligible Contributors	Employers, employees, and/or others	Employer only
Distributions	Tax-exempt benefits to employee, spouse, or tax dependents	Tax-exempt benefits to employees, spouses, tax dependents, or adult children under 27
Income Taxes— Employer Contributions	Not subject to federal income tax; subject to state income tax in AL, CA, NJ	Not subject to federal or state income tax
Income Taxes— Employee Contributions	Pre-tax payroll deductions or deductible on federal income return; subject to state income tax in AL, CA, NJ	Not applicable (employer contributions only)
Funding/Trust Required	Yes (must be held by bank, insurance company, or IRS-approved trustee)	Not required, self-administered or third-party administrator
Fund or Account Ownership	Employee	Employer
Rollover of Unused Funds at Year End	Yes	Yes, at employer's option
Rollover of Funds from Other Accounts	Yes—from another HSA; one-time rollover from IRA	No
Portable at Termination of Employment	Yes	No, other than COBRA

Elements	Health Savings Accounts (HSAs)	Health Reimbursement Arrangements (HRAs)
Minimum Deductible	Single—$1,250 Family—$2,500	None
Out-of-Pocket Maximum	Single—$6,350 Family—$12,700	None
Reported on W-2 as income to employee	No	No
Withdrawals for Non-Qualified Medical Expenses	Yes—subject to income tax and 20% penalty. No penalty after age 65.	No
Use to Pay for Insurance Premiums	Cannot use to pay health insurance premiums, with some exceptions	Can use to pay health insurance premiums, other than employer's major medical plan

A number of surveys, including Cigna's, show 20 percent growth rates in CDHPs in recent years, so there is no turning back from the consumer-driven transformation.

ENGAGED EMPLOYEES TEND TO BE HEALTHIER

On the behavior side, where the big payoffs reside, EBRI found adults in consumer-driven plans were more likely to be cost conscious, more likely to order generic drugs, less likely to smoke, more likely to exercise, and more likely to take advantage of health risk assessments, health promotions, and biometric screenings.

Not surprisingly, the engaged employees reported themselves to be in excellent or very good health. Once again, engagement is the key to health management.

Greg Scandlen, a health insurance guru, observed in his newsletter, "Policy people have been striving for decades to get patients to become more informed and engaged in their own care. It looks like the key to achieving that has been found."

The unstoppable march to health accounts portends a tipping point, when 15 percent of consumers—the leading-edge purchasers—move a whole market in favor of a product or service.

Similar to what happened with 401(k) plans versus traditional pension plans in the United States, it appears CDHPs have reached critical mass. The Obama administration, which down deep favors an eventual move to a nationalized single-payer health plan for all Americans, has not embraced HSAs, and consumer-driven plans, the fundamental building blocks for consumerism, but dares not undercut management tools that work so well to lower costs and have become so pervasive.

The charm of account-based health plans for employees is at least twofold:

- People like being in control of major parts of their lives. They are quite capable of buying homes, automobiles, computers, life insurance, and education for themselves and their children. Why would they not want to control their spending on health care?

■ Totals in HSA accounts, for which contributions, buildups, and withdrawals are tax-free, are becoming real assets. A few have reached six figures.

PROVIDE VALUE TO THE CUSTOMER

The widespread adoption and the resulting political safety of consumer-centric plans should give comfort to corporate managers contemplating a CDHP conversion. There is no longer any reason for corporate executives not to make the switch. The positive results from applying incentives to elicit healthy behaviors are proven, audited, and beyond debate.

In the broader scheme of things, the new army of some 40 million consumers is making a major impact on how health care is delivered. Consumers seek value, and that means they will be seeking out the providers that offer the best combination of service, price, and quality.

Health care providers are starting to dance to the music of an emerging marketplace. They are going lean by eliminating defects, infections, and waste. They are adjusting their value propositions to become patient-centric instead of production-centric. They are marketing to individuals, not just corporate payers. The best of the lot will be rewarded in the way that markets always reward top vendors—by keeping their customers and winning more volume.

Public policy gurus began scratching their heads in 2011 and 2012 when the hyperinflation trend lines in health care started to bend south to single-digit inflation, down from the double digits over the previous decade.

They need look no further than the critical mass of consumers who, empowered by their employers, are leading a grassroots revolution as they make individual decisions on treatments. Their collective actions are what is called a marketplace. What a novel idea.

LESSONS LEARNED

on Engaging Employees
as Consumers

☑ The surge toward consumer-driven health plans has become an unstoppable reform.

☑ Proven savings when employees become active consumers are 20 to 30 percent.

☑ Reform is all about behavior change.

☑ Financially engaged employees take better care of their family's health.

6

TRANSPARENCY:
ENTREPRENEURS SHINE LIGHT
ON PRICES, QUALITY

RICK FANTINI, vice president of human resources
at Menasha Corp., had a problem. The manufacturing and merchandising company had offered a
rich benefit plan for many years, but management could
see that the plan design would have to change as health
care costs continued their relentless climb. He didn't want
to surprise employees with a consumer-driven health plan
(CDHP) without also providing the tools to help them find
health care value.

"Providing a competitive benefit package is a differentiator for Menasha," he said. "But we also understand that offering consumer-directed or higher-deductible plans will help the company manage costs. Giving our employees access to a transparency information platform seemed like a logical first step."

The transparency tool allowed him and his employees to know where they should go for services. "Often," he said, "there was a lower-cost, similar-quality provider within a few miles, and sometimes just down the street."

Transparency platforms are absolutely necessary for intelligent consumerism to take hold, because providers are woeful at best, and misleading at worst, at volunteering real prices and meaningful quality ratings. Their allies in the insurance world haven't been much better.

Transparency platforms are absolutely necessary for intelligent consumerism to take hold, because providers are woeful at best, and misleading at worst, at volunteering real prices and meaningful quality ratings.

Despite no financial incentives to use the transparency tool, more than 20 percent of Menasha employees accessed the tool soon after adoption. At other companies, providing a modest financial incentive of $50 has increased utilization of transparent information in the weeks after launch.

Because the tools are so new, it is hard to estimate annual savings derived from employees now being able to shop for value. Providers of transparency solutions typically suggest that using their services will provide direct savings of 4 percent to 10 percent of a firm's overall health care bill.

Providers of transparency solutions typically suggest that using their services will provide direct savings of 4 to 10 percent of a firm's overall health care bill.

Menasha uses a transparency tool offered by Alithias Inc., a Wisconsin startup company. (Disclosure: I am an angel investor in the company.) But Alithias is not alone in rushing to fill the market gap for effective transparency tools. Other employers are being helped by a number of opportunistic entrepreneurs who have recognized that CDHPs are creating tens of millions of consumers who need market information.

STICKER SHOCK

Transparency websites are stripping away the camouflage surrounding the cost and quality of health care. Employees who make use of them are shocked to learn that prices can vary as much as 300 percent—or more—in the current, chaotic, inefficient "nonmarket" for health care. An MRI, for example, can be bought for less than $500 or more than $2,000. Purchasers salivate at the prospect of buying procedures at far lower prices.

Serigraph was at the transparency ramparts eight years ago when our head of human resources, Linda Buntrock, dug into our self-insured claims data to elicit price ranges on 10 common procedures. With the help of Anthem, our claims administrator, she proved it could be done.

Her intranet site, MedSave, expanded to shine a spotlight on almost 100 procedures. She further developed it to include A, B, and C quality ratings and volumes performed at different health facilities. Our co-workers at Serigraph check our MedSave website before signing up for an elective medical procedure so they can find the best value. They and the company have saved hundreds of thousands of dollars since offering transparency.

Alithias founder Ross Bjella modeled his platform after the Serigraph MedSave concept and has sold it to major self-insured companies in eastern Wisconsin, where he has been able to access claims data.

These companies are winning savings on elective procedures, but have learned that transparency alone is not enough. Coupled, though, with significant incentives to make smart buys of procedures, the clarity tools work wonders.

Health Care Shopping on the Go

Alithias has a mobile app with which consumers can look up prices and quality at any time. Just punch in "knee arthroscopy" or "colonoscopy" and up comes a menu of

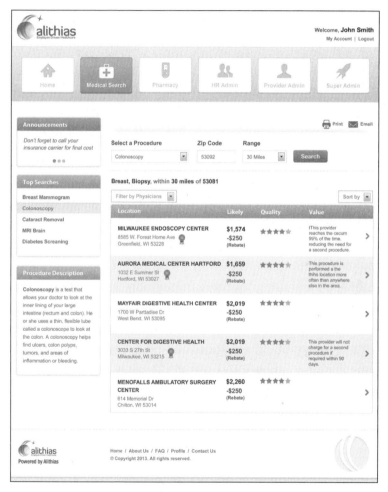

Typical page from Alithias transparency tool

options in the area, including a link that connects the user directly to the provider, making it easier for high-quality providers to get more patients.

"Shining a bright light on medical prices and quality can have a major impact on the affordability of care for employers and employees," said Bjella. "Why should employees pay two, three, or four times the charges for services when there are options by providers who do a great job on both quality and price?"

"Price transparency is clearly the topic du jour and will be for a while," stated Andrea Caballero, program director for San Francisco–based Catalyst for Payment Reform, a nonprofit group representing large private and public employers. "When provided meaningful price and quality information, 80 percent of consumers select the highest value provider," she said.

Similar bright lights are exposing the best deals on prices for pharmaceuticals, both brand and generic.

The trick for employers is to get employees who need a procedure to use the site and to use the best providers. The best method is plain old cash.

Serigraph's MedSave plan offers $2,000 in cash to coworkers who select a Center of Value for a joint replacement of coronary bypass. It's $500 for a smart purchase of a colonoscopy and $250 for an MRI. (We had one couple go in together for their colonoscopies. Now, that's togetherness. And no, we are not worried that the rebate will lead to overutilization of colonoscopies.)

Other companies use the stick instead of the carrot. Employees pay more if they pick low-value providers, those with high prices and low quality.

DISCLOSING INFORMATION TO CONSUMERS, PROVIDING ADVOCATES

Insurance companies and health care companies are also releasing some price and effectiveness data. UnitedHealthcare, for example, rolled out its myHealthcare Cost Estimator in 2012. It has the virtue of having its price information based on its actual contracted prices. It lets consumers see exactly what their out-of-pocket expenses will be for a treatment.

Insurance company websites tend to be clunky, but at least some consumer information is out there.

After a procedure has been billed, the Explanation of Benefits from insurers (EOBs) often serves to confuse consumers more than enlighten them. The independent transparency vendors solve that issue with user-friendly websites that show employees exactly what comes from their pockets.

One of the latest to bring a transparency product forward is an Iowa firm named Auxiant, with offices in Milwaukee and Madison, Wisconsin. It offers a product called FocusHealth that gives hospitals and clinics an overall composite score for value. It also drills down to price, quality, and value for separate procedures. The value score combines the cost and quality scores.

Take spinal surgery in one market as an example. Auxiant, using claims data, rates Aurora Medical Center in Hartford, Wisconsin, in the 83rd percentile in the state (100 is tops) for cost performance and 74th for quality. Nearby Community Memorial Hospital in Menomonee Falls rates 70th and 43rd, respectively. Competing Froedtert Health/St. Joseph's Hospital in West Bend scores 57th and 68th. So, the top value in this small market, represented by a green thumbs-up icon, goes to Aurora for that procedure. What consumer wouldn't pay attention to such ratings before ordering a procedure? If they don't, they should.

Another lever that employers can use for steerage to best buys is an advocate. The advocate can be a benefits specialist, an on-site medical team member, or a contracted firm in that business.

The consumer advocate works with an employee to help with assessment of whether the procedure is necessary, including getting second opinions; choice of providers using a transparency tool; coordination during the episode of care; follow-up rehabilitation; and billings and payment plans.

Again, though, the trick is getting a high level of steerage to the best provider in the emerging marketplace for health care. That's where the major dollars are saved.

Types of Transparency

Among the other entrepreneurial companies that have jumped into the race to provide consumer information about health care is Castlight, which raised $180 million in venture capital money in Silicon Valley. It is selling its service to major corporations.

Though reticent about disclosing its customer list, Castlight cited USA Mobility, which reported a 70 percent usage for the Castlight transparency tool right out of the chute.

"It's like taking the veil off the bride," said Bonnie Culp, head of human resources at USA Mobility.

Each transparency vendor has different features. Some, like Compass Professional Health Services out of Texas, include patient advocacy and navigation services for employees as they make elective treatment decisions. Compass clients report significant savings.

Castlight said it intends to drill down to quality performance at the doctor level. The Alliance, a collaboration of 180 employers in Madison, Wisconsin, is also working to report on quality at the physician level as an addition to its "Quality Counts" transparency model.

Mutual of Omaha, a nationwide insurance company, has stepped into the fray with a product called "mpower360" that empowers employees with a full range of tools: cost and quality scores for different procedures at different facilities; alerts on the best deals; scheduling of appointments; a clear explanation of the split of costs between employer and employee and what employees will pay from their health account or out of pocket; balances on the health account before and after a procedure; an error alert when there is an overcharge by a provider; and online bill payments. Mutual sells itself as a "navigator" to help employees make the best buys.

"Employees can manage all of their health care in one spot," said Todd Covert, Mutual's head of strategy.

Here's a rundown by Mutual on a visit by "Tina" to an El Camino, California, clinic for an obstetric exam. The sticker price for the office visit was $180. The insurance discount was $79, for a net charge of $101. The employee copay was a flat $20.

The accompanying ultrasound test was billed at a sticker price of $285. The insurance discount was $110, leaving $175 to be paid. Tina had not met her deductible, so the cost was all hers.

The overall "sticker" price for Tina's visit, all-in, was $465. That's way too much for a simple visit, but that's what uninsured people pay. Tina's portion, spelled out clearly, was $195. Going in, Tina knew exactly what she was being charged, what her company was paying, and what she would pay from her HSA or her pocket.

The price companies pay for transparency services range from $2 to $5 per employee per month. That is a small fee for an employer to pay compared to the potential savings. The savings from one smartly purchased knee replacement alone could more than pay for the annual cost of the transparency tool at a mid-size company.

Comparing Hospitals—and Even Auditing Them

Consumer Reports dropped a bombshell when it came out with ratings for Wisconsin hospitals. It was based on information voluntarily submitted by some providers to the Wisconsin Collaborative on Health Care Quality. The comparisons were eye-opening.

Consumer Reports used its iconic red and black dots for displaying hospital records on five dimensions: safety, bloodstream infections, avoiding readmissions, drug information, and use of electronic medical records.

The most positive red dots went to Bellin Memorial Hospital in Green Bay. Its safety score was 74 on a scale of 100, and it had a full, positive red dot for low infections and a half red dot for readmissions.

Community Memorial Hospital in the Milwaukee market recorded a 48 for safety, a half red dot for electronic records and a half black negative dot for readmissions. St. Joseph's, another small hospital in that market, was not rated, except for half black dots for readmits and infections. Aurora Health, the state's largest system, chose not to provide data to the Collaborative.

The Collaborative and *Consumer Reports* have a lot of holes to fill in their reports. Many Wisconsin hospitals were not rated or only partially rated. But their work still is a great step forward for pushing providers to higher levels of value and for helping consumers make good decisions.

Consumer Reports has issued similar statewide findings in Minnesota and Massachusetts.

If they really wanted to manage the health care supply chain, corporate payers could be much more aggressive. They could solve the problem of insufficient quality information by simply auditing their health care vendors as they do other vendors.

Serigraph's customers do regular audits of our operations. We audit our vendors. Winning and keeping business depends on good scores. Why not health care audits?

Ultimate price transparency comes from what is known as bundled prices. Corporate payers are demanding all-in prices for an episode of care, and they are getting them.

The lowest bundled price we've seen at Serigraph for knee replacements is $27,500. If the price for a knee replacement moves to $30,000 next year, we will spot the increase immediately and have a serious conversation with the vendor about the reason for the price hike. In the Milwaukee market, knee replacement prices range from $27,500 to $70,586, with a median of $44,422. That's an incredible variation.

Ultimate price transparency comes from what is known as bundled prices. Corporate payers are demanding all-in prices for procedures, and they are getting them.

Prior to bundled prices, hospitals could slip through price increases because the bills were piecemeal and incomprehensible. It was a fog, just like the providers liked it.

This is just the beginning of transparency reform in the nation.

MORE STATES DRAWN TO THE TRANSPARENCY TREND

More than twenty states are building consolidated claims data bases, including New York, which made public the charges on 1,400 procedures in late 2013. Wisconsin got an early start. Its Wisconsin Health Information Organization (WHIO) began an All-Payer Claims Database (APCD) six years ago and has two-thirds of Wisconsin residents included. It can compare episodes of care for cost, quality, and utilization.

It is WHIO's intention to dive into physician level reporting in 2014, which would be a major advance for full transparency. Consumers need to know what's happening at the doctor level, too. Not all doctors are created equal when it comes to outcomes.

At the hospital level, its "Datamart" is now available for self-analysis by providers and for shopping comparison by payers looking for transparency. WHIO could also sell its data to transparency entrepreneurs.

A battle royal has emerged in the nation over who owns the claims data. Health insurers like UnitedHealthcare resist mightily access to their claims databases, arguing that such data is confidential.

The insurers say they have confidentiality clauses in their contracts with providers, and they do.

But let's get real. The data also belongs to the payers, especially self-insured payers. They write the checks. Such payments are the data points in the claims databases.

Isn't it absurd for an insurer to tell a payer it can't have its own data?

Isn't it absurd for an insurer to tell a payer it can't have its own data?

It is understandable that insurers would want to keep claims data and discounts locked up. It's their prime intellectual property. Said Julie Bartels, former WHIO CEO, "It all comes down to who owns the data."

Said Matt Olson, who develops software for Alithias, "They sell you on their discounts, and then they won't let you see the data to validate the discounts." Tongue firmly in cheek, he called the current system "translucency."

Nonetheless, in the end, payers will get the claims data if they demand it.

Third-Party Administrators

Smaller Third-Party Administrators, or TPAs, have been more cooperative. They are trying to gain market share among payers by being on the payer's side, so they release claims data that is stripped of personal identification. The aggregated data can be used to good purpose, while privacy of patients is preserved.

Alithias gets claims dumps, for instance, from two small TPAs in Wisconsin, and that became the raw material for transparency in the eastern part of the state.

It is just a matter of time until the hospital systems with the lowest prices and best quality ratings start posting them on the transparency websites. It will be a business generator for them.

The less-qualified vendors, on the other hand, will avoid publishing results. And they will inevitably lose market share, as they should.

Think about the market size for transparency services. There are 40 million new consumers with HRAs or HSAs, people who want to make value-based purchases. That number grows to an estimated 70 million if all high-deductible plans are tallied.

Payers, both employers and employees, won't stand for the incomprehensible bills of the past. There is way too much money at stake to tolerate foggy pricing.

The cork is out of the bottle on consumer health care information, and it is not going back in. Payers, both employers and employees, won't stand for the incomprehensible bills of the past. There is way too much money at stake to tolerate foggy pricing.

LESSONS LEARNED
on Transparency

☑ Payers—employers and employees—must demand openness on price and quality.

☑ Prices vary wildly.

☑ Cost savings from steerage to Centers of Value for elective procedures are huge—as much as 50 percent or more.

☑ Employers need to use incentives to steer employees to the best providers. Cash works well.

☑ Advocates, such as benefits specialists or on-site health professionals, can help greatly with steerage.

☑ Payers should demand the release of their claims data from insurers or TPAs.

7

CENTERS OF VALUE:
COMPANIES MOVE BUSINESS

W HEN LOWE'S CUT A DEAL with the well-
regarded Cleveland Clinic in 2010 for cost-
effective cardiac surgeries, it was part of a
megatrend toward value-based purchasing.

Large employers are shaping a real marketplace for
health care by moving business to Centers of Value, places
where value means a winning trio of service, quality, and
price. At a Center of Value, employers and their employees can buy world-class quality at attractive, all-inclusive,
bundled prices.

The backdrop for these strategic, market-disrupting decisions is a crazy quilt of prices in the health care industry. Chaotic and elusive prices can vary more than 300 percent in a region.

THE APPROACH TO ELECTIVE SURGERIES

Joining Lowe's in buying elective surgeries from the Cleveland Clinic are Boeing, Walmart, Kohl's, Rich Products Corp., and Alliance Oil.

PepsiCo cut a similar deal in 2011 with The Johns Hopkins Hospital in Baltimore for cost-effective cardiac and joint replacement surgeries. PepsiCo, with a quarter-million insured lives, got more than a 25 percent participation rate for such elective surgeries in its first year. The company covers travel costs and waives all out-of-pocket charges for its people utilizing this arrangement.

"These programs are designed to help our employees and their families to live healthier lives and ensure a high level of workforce support, which, in turn, helps PepsiCo be a successful company," said Bruce Monte, senior director of health and benefits.

Look at it another way: Why would employers allow employees to be operated on at an inferior hospital? It would border on unethical.

In 2012, Lowe's expanded its contract with Cleveland Clinic to include spinal surgeries. It wouldn't be enlarging the relationship if the cardiac outsourcing weren't working beautifully.

Bob Ihrie, Lowe's senior vice president, said, "Having the correct diagnoses, combined with surgery by the undisputed leaders in the field, will produce the highest-quality outcomes."

Lowe's, which has 200,000 members in its self-insured plan, reported participation beyond expectations, but gave no actual numbers. Employees see lower out-of-pocket costs and have their entire trip expenses covered by the company.

"Having the correct diagnoses, combined with surgery by the undisputed leaders in the field, will produce the highest-quality outcomes."
—BOB IHRIE, LOWE'S SENIOR VICE PRESIDENT

Some employers, such as Serigraph, want the savings and outcomes so much that they make elective surgeries free to plan members willing to travel to a Center of Value. The members pay no deductible or coinsurance charges.

This disruptive business model is obviously working for Cleveland Clinic. It is picking up volume. Of its 4,200 heart surgeries in 2012, half came from outside Ohio. Added volume is the reward for a value proposition that works for customers.

"If you're a large employer, with facilities across the nation, you see great variations in health care quality," said Michael McMillan, Cleveland Clinic's head of marketing. "How do you reduce those variations? By getting people into the places where they do a great job. When you do that, you not only improve quality, but cost."

Because of its early success with direct contracts with employers in the private sector, Cleveland Clinic is working to offer similar plans in pain management, orthopedics, and neurosurgery. It is also cutting deals with other hospitals around the country to lend its brand and management expertise to their heart programs. Columbia St. Mary's in Milwaukee is an example. It will team with Cleveland to win heart surgery business on a value basis.

McMillan said the market's hunger for best-outcome, bundled-price medical care is intense and growing.

THE VALUE PLAN

The search for value began at least a decade ago. SC Johnson sent its in-house doctors to uncover Centers of Value for back, joint, and heart surgeries. It found three each and then strongly urged employees to go there. Johnson wanted its people to enjoy the best outcomes and low prices. The company put in a disincentive for lower-value choices, namely a doubling of the out-of-pocket maximum costs if an employee went outside its value circle for surgery.

At Serigraph, we use a carrot instead of a stick. When Dave Wagner, one of our tooling managers, required a total knee replacement, he consulted with our benefit experts and selected one of our providers of choice. For that, he received a cash reward of $2,000.

Said Wagner after the surgery, and returning to work part-time just three weeks later: "This was win-win-win. One, together, we saved money by moving my surgery from one hospital that raised its prices just before the operation to our Center of Value and its bundled price. Two, my out-of-pocket was minimized. And three, the results were more than I hoped for."

Even better, some payers are now asking for, and getting, warranties on surgeries.

The Orthopaedic Hospital of Wisconsin (OHOW), which has confidence in its processes and outcomes, took the challenge and has given warranties. That means re-admits and do-overs for surgery are on the house.

If this seems too much to ask or offer, ask what other industry would be able to charge a customer for its mistakes?

Imagine: a low price, coupled with a warranty—what a good buy! An OHOW knee replacement, for example, can be bought for $27,500. That's all-in for a three-night stay. No extra bills for anesthesiology, drugs, scans, or recovery.

Further, OHOW managers report an infection rate at a very low 0.2 percent. That's a metric that ought to rank high in any patient's choice of where to go.

That stands in sharp contrast to hospitals in general. According to the Centers for Disease Control and

Prevention, 5 to 10 percent of patients pick up a preventable infection in the hospital, and nearly 100,000 people die from one each year.

Steerage to hospitals that minimize infections and other errors is the right thing to do.

PRICE VERSUS QUALITY

Some recent research points to an emerging inverse correlation between price and quality. If you are looking for an elective surgery, consider looking for the cheapest place. Cheaper is better. That, of course, flies in the face of conventional wisdom that high prices mean high quality.

If you are looking for an elective surgery, consider looking for the cheapest place.

The misunderstanding about the price/quality dynamics is especially strong in union circles. Union leaders have bargained over the years for very costly plans, some up in the "Cadillac" stratosphere of $27,500 or more per employee. They view any cost reduction as a retreat from what they bargained so hard to get.

That's simply a wrong-headed conclusion. Pure and simple, high prices are just a sign of mismanagement or undermanagement. Paying excessive prices has many consequences. For example, high benefit costs usually result in lower or no raises for workers, because pay and benefits interact in a package. In other words, if benefits get out of control, wages suffer.

High benefit costs usually result in lower or no raises for workers, because pay and benefits interact in a package. In other words, if benefits get out of control, wages suffer.

The first breach in that wall of misunderstanding came when *The Wall Street Journal* investigated the prices and quality of radiology scans. Its reporting showed no correlation between prices and quality.

Then in 2012, the Wisconsin Collaborative for Health Care Quality, after nearly a decade of gathering claims data and doing analysis, blew the doors off conventional wisdom. It tracked the relationship between cost and quality on three pneumonia treatments and three heart procedures. Eureka! Some of the highest-quality hospitals also delivered the lowest prices—cheaper is better.

Look at the accompanying quadrant analysis from the Collaborative. It shows that a good number of the highest-quality providers for heart care were also the least expensive. They are in the upper left quadrant.

HEART ATTACK CARE HOSPITAL CHARGES AND QUALITY COMPARISON

This quadrant analysis represents a comparison of heart at-tack (also called AMI or acute myocardial infarction) quality of care and charges. The purpose of this analysis is to attempt to quantify the value each hospital provides when caring for patients with heart attacks.

The quality score is a composite number that takes into account how well a hospital performed in giving the recom-mended care proven to give the best results to most adults with a heart attack. The charges are risk adjusted to account for differences in patients such as severity of illness and risk of death.

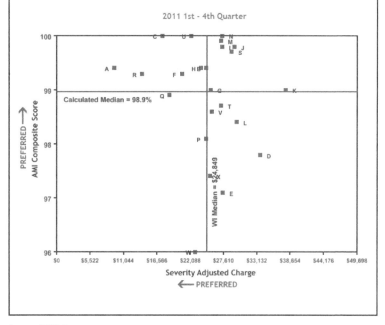

SOURCE: WCHQ.org

106

How Volume Plays into Price

This correlation between high quality and low price is counterintuitive. But not if you do a deeper dig.

First, it is generally accepted that there is a direct correlation between volume and quality. The more procedures a medical team performs, the better it gets. The better it gets, the more surgeries it attracts.

Further, it's a marketplace working like it should work. The high-quality providers get rewarded with more customers. It is the obligation of C-suite purchasers to make sure that happens.

Second, the highest-quality providers are often the ones that are the most serious about lean disciplines. That is the body of managerial science that has transformed the manufacturing world.

It started with Toyota 30 years ago as it began its climb to the top of the global automotive world. Perceived quality in the eye of the consumer has carried the day for Toyota and other Asian carmakers to a commanding position. Fortunately for the United States, there is now a growing cadre of health care providers who are applying Toyota-like philosophies to their operations. It's about time.

Lean strategies concentrate on these principles:

- Always, always listen first to the voice of the customer; in health care, that's the patient.
- Drive out every form of waste, defined as anything that doesn't add value for the customer.

- Strive for zero defects, such as no infections in an operating room.
- Educate and fully engage every co-worker in continual improvement, in lasting solutions to root cause problems.
- Hold deep respect for co-workers and their efforts.
- Use sophisticated statistical tools and methods to help problem-solving teams get to enduring answers.
- Bake the solutions into standard practices.
- Never end the lean journey. Its tenet of humility holds that continuous improvements are always possible.

These transformational methods have allowed high-wage U.S. manufacturers to compete on cost and quality with low-wage competitors from abroad. They have enabled a return of some work from China.

The race to be the leanest of the lean does great things for consumers. Remember the bad old days when a car had to be traded at 60,000 miles? Today, it is not unusual for consumers to drive cars for 200,000 miles, some even 300,000. Lean disciplines accomplished that.

Similarly, lean methodology is how some leading-edge hospitals literally have driven most infections from their operating rooms.

Here are three lean examples cited in a Mayo Clinic report:

- Pediatric surgeons at Seattle Children's Hospital vie to perform surgery at the new Bellevue Clinic and Surgery Center because of the efficient flow for patients, families, and the care team. Operations start when scheduled 99 percent of the time. More than 90 percent of patients and families give the Bellevue Surgery Center a 9 or 10 rating for overall care.

- ThedaCare, a Wisconsin-based integrated health system, reduced inpatient total cost of care by 25 percent while improving patient satisfaction to nearly 100 percent, rating their care 5 on a scale of 5. For five years running, there were no medication reconciliation errors for patients in hospital units. Care teams include a pharmacist.

- The staff of the otolaryngology department of the Christie Clinic in Champaign, Illinois, begins each day with a huddle to identify problems and discuss potential solutions. In less than one year after starting the huddles, waiting time for appointments decreased by 28 percent, departmental capacity improved by 10 percent with no increase in head count, and patient satisfaction increased from 4.3 to 4.7 on a 5-point scale.

In contrast, hospitals in general do poorly in national ratings for customer satisfaction.

There is also a service quotient in the value proposition for Centers of Value. Why shouldn't a woman get the results from a mammogram before the end of the day? Follow-up and treatment can start faster if there is a questionable finding. In such a case, service and quality are intertwined.

Why shouldn't tests be conducted at the beginning of an office visit at a clinic and then made available to doctor and patient before the end of the visit? This is not without treatment consequences.

Such service is being delivered every day by health care systems that are on the lean journey.

The quest for quality becomes a virtuous circle. Higher quality begets more volume; less waste begets lower costs and prices; lower prices and high quality beget more volume and higher profits.

Higher quality begets more volume; less waste begets lower costs and prices; lower prices and high quality beget more volume and higher profits.

Remember a business truism: extra sales volume at the margin has a disproportionately positive impact on the bottom line. A volume pickup boosts the profits of any company sharply, and the reverse is also true for poor hospitals that lose business.

This wholesome marketplace dynamic only works if purchasers and their employees are willing to shake the status quo and seek high-value providers. They have to move the business. They have to reward the Centers of Value.

"We are increasingly seeing employers act on information for purchasing," said Cheryl DeMars, executive director of The Alliance, a cooperative of 184 employers in Wisconsin and Illinois.

The Alliance has its own claims database, so it knows that prices on fixing torn knee cartilage can vary almost $8,000 in a 33-mile radius.

"We want employees to organically seek better value," stated DeMars. If they don't, the best providers actually lose revenue because of a perverse dynamic in today's busted business model. By keeping people well, the best providers lose treatments in their clinics and hospitals. By cutting down hospital stays, they also lose revenue.

THE POWER OF LEAN

John Toussaint, former CEO of ThedaCare Center for Healthcare Value in Appleton, Wisconsin, and an evangelist for lean disciplines in health care, is making the bet that lean providers will win in the long term, as payers shift to value-based purchasing.

That has started to happen. Smart corporate payers, acting in the best interests of their companies, their employees, and investors, are actually moving business to the best centers. Again, those providers are often the ones that do the best job of controlling sepsis, the leading cause of hospital deaths, and reducing readmits, pressure ulcers, and drug errors.

George Halvorson, CEO of Kaiser Permanente, has made reduction of sepsis, a toxic response to hospital infections, a national cause. "Sepsis is the number-one cause of death in American hospitals," he says. "Your chance of dying from a sepsis infection can triple if you choose a hospital that doesn't have a good sepsis response team."

From just a handful of lean leaders five years ago, Toussaint rounded up 66 hospitals for his lean leadership movement. That's about 1 percent of all U.S. hospitals as of 2013.

Imagine the impact of lean in health care if these examples were the warp and woof of medicine across clinics and hospital in the United States. There's a long way to go, and only intense pressure from value purchasers can make lean go faster in health care.

"We are now trying to manage the demand" for lean education as other hospital CEOs race to adopt lean disciplines, Toussaint said.

That's most encouraging. These lean providers will be the survivors as the disruptive new business model takes root.

They also will be winners as medicine goes global.

MEDICAL TOURISM

Though most payers in the private sector have not pursued inexpensive surgeries in foreign countries, individual American consumers flock across the border for elective surgeries. That is especially true of uncovered procedures, like plastic surgery. And it is true for people without adequate insurance. They can, for example, buy a new hip for $5,000 in India versus $25,000 or much more in the United States.

It is only a matter of time before corporate purchasers turn medicine into a global marketplace by tapping into hospitals overseas. But that will only happen if those institutions show top-quality ratings.

Value-based health care is not just about price.

LESSONS LEARNED
on Centers of Value

☑ Cut deals with high-value hospitals for elective procedures.

☑ Create incentives for employees to travel to Centers of Value.

☑ Ask for warranties on surgeries.

☑ Understand the emerging inverse correlation between quality and cost, and the favorable correlation between volume of procedures and quality.

☑ Send your business to lean hospitals and clinics.

☑ Ask hospitals about infection rates.

8

RESTRUCTURED PRICING:
COMPANIES DEMAND
BETTER MODELS

I F SAFEWAY CAN OFFER its employees the choice of five accredited endoscopy shops where they can buy colonoscopies for $1,500 or less, and they are within a reasonable distance, why would the grocery company ever pay more? Why indeed. So Safeway doesn't.

Safeway and a number of other payers have developed what is called Reference-Based Pricing (RBP) to keep a lid on health care costs. They simply say to their employees, "You can go anywhere you want, and we will cover the costs up to $1,500. If you pick an uncompetitive clinic, and the charge is higher than that, fine, but you pay the difference out of your pocket."

This "cap" is one of the many forms of payment reform that are coming into play across the country as purchasers clamp down on the incomprehensible pricing policies that have allowed the health care industry to engage in undisciplined increases year in and year out for decades.

Medical providers have had the luxury of operating in a world where, heretofore, there was neither market discipline on prices nor government regulation of prices, the norm in utility kinds of businesses. It has been a no-man's-land where anything goes for charges. How else do you explain price variations of 300 percent or more for the same procedure? That wild variation is prevalent for many treatments across the country.

It has been a no-man's-land where anything goes for charges. How else do you explain price variations of 300 percent or more for the same procedure?

One software expert who has spent years trying to make sense of the messy data coming out of claims databases commented, "It's so screwed up that I have to believe it has to be on purpose."

His skepticism is not unwarranted. Prices for procedures in other industrialized countries run one-third or less of U.S. prices.

ALL-IN PRICING

Payment reforms depend, first and foremost, on transparency for value. That is the combination of service, price, and quality. But transparency alone is not enough. Employers and employees need to act on transparent information. Nothing, for instance, is more transparent and actionable than a reference-based price. It is unequivocal at Safeway what a colonoscopy should cost, namely no more than $1,500, all-in.

Once that price was set, some providers actually came in under $1,500.

That total charge is what is called a bundled or fixed price, another piece of the payment reform movement. More and more payers are demanding all-in prices for medical episodes, and they are getting them. They allow no add-on bills for related services.

Some very big players are following suit. WellPoint, the second-largest health insurer in the country, teamed up with the California Public Employees' Retirement System, known as CalPERS, on a pilot program to cap prices on hip and knee replacements at $30,000.

It worked famously. In the end, 54 hospital facilities participated, including leaders like Cedars-Sinai Medical

Center and Stanford Hospital & Clinics. Prices dropped to $28,695 in 2011, according to one analysis, and to $27,149 in 2012, according to another.

A CalPERS spokesperson said the organization had been paying anywhere from $15,000 to $110,000 per replacement. Only in the crazy world of medical prices would you find a difference of almost a hundred grand for the same procedure.

"It's a symptom of the completely irrational pricing structure hospitals have," said Ann Boynton, a CalPERS benefit executive, when introducing the caps to members. The RBP cap saved CalPERS $5.5 million over two years.

In an astounding initiative, WellPoint has told major employers that it will roll out the RBP program to 900 different procedures in 2014.

"It's a race to value," said Dr. Samuel Nussbaum, chief medical officer for WellPoint, about the payment reforms. The broader program includes lab tests and imaging scans. MRIs, as an example, can be bought for $525, or even lower, compared to the $2,000 or $4,000 commonly charged by some big medical systems.

WellPoint reported that its pilot program with capped prices showed that hospitals in the RBP program had lower rates of hospital-acquired infections and readmissions—further proof that there is no correlation between price and quality. Put another way, providers that have their acts together drive out waste and process defects. That means lower costs, which in turn allows lower prices.

Other big players are following the lead of Safeway, CalPERS, and WellPoint. Aetna started with caps on 11 outpatient procedures that it offered to medium and large employers. Cigna ran a pilot in 2011 and cited mixed results. Kroger Co., another large grocery chain, has put an $800 cap on MRI and CT scans.

While only a small percentage of private companies were using RBP in 2013, surveys show many more moving in that direction. Why wouldn't they?

Price reductions of major proportions via caps constitute genuine deflation. It will be shock therapy for hospital executives who will have to figure out how to meet the new market prices or lose business.

Note: when fixed prices are offered to payers, it takes insurance plans partially out of the picture. The insurance discounts, which are at the heart of their current business model, no longer apply.

Bundled prices shouldn't be that hard; it just takes effective cost accounting. Many hospital systems admit to being weak in that basic business discipline.

Think about this incongruity. The purported strategy of the big systems is to deliver integrated care. If care is integrated, why not the bills, too? How hard can it be, for instance, to put a fixed price on a vaginal delivery? That's a routine, repeatable process that lends itself to a single price.

How Did We Get in This Mess?

Let's take a step back for perspective. How did medical pricing get so screwed up in the first place? As you might suspect, the massive confusion and long list of unintended consequences started with the federal government. When significant money started to flow from federal coffers via the Medicare and Medicaid programs in the early 1980s, the feds set out to standardize payments. It created classifications called Current Procedure Terminology, or CPT codes. Essentially, to be billed and reimbursed, every procedure done by a doctor, clinic, or hospital has to fit into a CPT classification.

The feds decided they didn't have the technical expertise to rate procedures, so they asked the American Medical Association (AMA), which represents doctors, to take over the work.

Daniel Palestrant, a doctor and entrepreneur, wrote a paper in 2012 and blogs on the subject to tell what happened next:

> The AMA quickly realized that if they could get the government to grant them a monopoly on the definitions, they could update the CPT codes anytime and force everyone to pay them a licensing fee for each time they updated the codes, which they began to do every year like clockwork.
>
> They turned CPT codes into a necessity that they owned and that everybody needed to utilize—including the insurance and hospital establishment—if they wanted

to participate in payment transactions for medical services.

Not knowing any better, the government granted the AMA an exclusive license, making CPT codes the only way a physician could be paid by either insurance companies or the government itself.

The AMA realized that they could make far more money on royalties from the CPT codes (as long as hospitals, insurance companies and physicians are forced to use them) than they ever could make representing the actual interests of their physician membership.

Palestrant puts AMA revenues in the hundreds of millions of dollars just from CPT royalties.

Consider the perverse outcomes that flow from the CPT straightjacket on medical pricing:

- Medical bills and EOBs (Explanation of Benefits from health insurers), often with multiple line items for different CPT codes, are incomprehensible to the average patient. Even company chief financial officers can't figure out the bills. The pricing fog starts with the CPT codes.
- Gamesmanship is rampant, as consultants teach providers how to "upcode" for higher payments.
- Medical professionals on the front line literally can't tell a patient how much a medical treatment is going to cost.
- Doctors argue that the standardization inhibits innovation, because codes don't exist for the new

methods and take a long time for the AMA to develop and disseminate.

- Codes are oriented to procedures, not to health.
- Doctors argue that some medicine should be customized, not standardized, but the system doesn't allow for that.
- The complex coding process creates huge administrative overheads on the part of payers and providers, diverting resources from actual care.
- The bureaucratic coding nightmare causes delays in payments, which adds another level of inefficiency to the health care industry.
- The complex bills make side-by-side comparisons of health care prices difficult.

So, the obvious question for the private sector becomes: why would we subject ourselves to such a convoluted pricing system? It's one thing for the government to tie itself to the CPT monster, but why should we?

Again, remember the golden rule. Companies are the purchasers, and the payers usually get to set the pricing rules. So why don't we in the private sector just scrap the convoluted CPT system?

As you might guess, that's exactly what's happening—in a number of ways. Reference-Based Pricing, which incorporates bundled pricing, goes right around the AMA monopoly.

Here's what Booz & Company reported in a report entitled, "Bundled Care: The Voice of the Consumer":

Perhaps the clearest sign of momentum is the move by some influential national employers to offer bundles as part of their employees' health coverage. Beginning in 2013, Walmart, the world's largest private employer, will collaborate with leading providers such as Mayo Clinic, Cleveland Clinic, and Geisinger Health System to offer bundled care for a number of common procedures, including heart surgery. Through this offering, Walmart employees can elect to receive care at top facilities with no deductible or coinsurance cost. Walmart will also cover the cost of airfare and lodging for the employee and one companion.

Walmart determined that doing all of this would be more cost-effective than having employees receive care at local, non-specialist facilities. In this virtuous cycle, designated healthcare organizations gain volume in treating certain conditions, allowing them to fine-tune their medical processes and reduce waste.

USING MEDICARE RATES AS THE BASELINE

In another payment departure, Cincinnati companies like Ilsco, an electrical connector manufacturer, and Home City Ice have used the Medicare pricing system to their advantage. They have adopted a new plan, called TrueCost, that sets payments at Medicare rates plus a 40 percent "provider bonus."

Providers are resisting because Medicare uses its government power to install what amounts to price controls. That means low reimbursements. Medicare rates are generally viewed as close to a hospital or clinic's real costs. If that's true, a 40 percent markup should be sufficient to make a profit.

How can providers object? If they are accepting Medicare rates from the government, how can they not accept higher prices in the private sector? Logic aside, they surely will fight linkage to low Medicare reimbursement.

Another large company uses a cap of 175 percent of Medicare if an employee chooses to go outside of network.

Palestrant and his partner, Dr. Adam Sharp, have developed a whole new game plan for medical pricing. It's called "direct dynamic pricing," essentially an online auction for medical procedures.

Their company, par8o, signed a preliminary deal with the MGM Grand Hotel & Casino in Las Vegas that will allow the casino's employees to put out a request for quote on medical procedures. The providers will show a baseline price on procedures, like knee or hip replacements, on par8o's transparency site, but then, as with an auction, have the ability to bid even lower if they have open capacity.

Much like Priceline for the travel industry, par8o enables consumers to make spot health care buys at lower than standard, advertised prices.

Much like Priceline for the travel industry, par8o enables consumers to make spot health care buys at lower than standard, advertised prices.

Said Palestrant: "More sophisticated, self-insured payers are moving toward more ways to pay. They want to set up direct pay channels."

Think about this potential scenario. An employee goes to his company's benefits expert to get advice on where to go for a knee replacement. The benefits specialist pulls up the transparency tool. It shows that the best value is a new knee for $27,500 at a clinic where the infection rate is close to zero.

She and the employee agree to use this Center of Value, even though it's 30 miles away. She punches an icon that says "Order." A pre-surgery meeting is automatically scheduled.

Everyone's happy. The clinic gets the business. The employee gets a rebate of $1,000 for making a value-based decision. The self-insured employer saves $10,000 or more from a regional average on knee replacements. The transparency provider gets a 3 percent "click-through" commission, which the clinic is more than happy to pay for getting "a head on a bed."

The only unhappy party is the low-value provider. It lost the business because its quality was not up to standards and its price was too high.

A positive epilogue, of course, is that the loser hospital gets its act together on quality and price and lives to compete another day. It's either that or a business obituary, at least for that procedure.

Such a pricing system, when broadly adopted, will unleash the powers of the marketplace and rationalize prices.

Gone will be the price variations of 300 percent or more. Gone will be the third-party payers, the middlemen. Gone will be the pricing fog. Pricing transactions will be in concert with supply and demand.

Such a pricing system, when broadly adopted, will unleash the powers of the marketplace and rationalize prices... Pricing transactions will be in concert with supply and demand.

PRICE CONTROLS ON PRESCRIPTIONS

Similarly, BidRx, a venture based in Oshkosh, Wisconsin, is using direct dynamic pricing for pharmaceuticals. BidRx allows a patient and doctor to go to its website, call up any prescription drug, look at a baseline price, check out all the valid substitutes, including generics and their lower prices, ask for an auctioned price, punch a button, and order at the low, "dynamic" price. The inexpensive drug arrives by mail a few days later from the low-bid pharmacy.

Another similar site, RxCut, offered by Free For All Inc., also yields savings. For instance, Lamisil, which is prescribed for nail fungus, goes for $622.85 per month at one pharmacy. But the generic, terbinafine, goes for $64.13 at the top and $16.31 at the low end.

Smart employers have made generic drugs free to employees because they are so cost-effective.

Ralph Kalies, founder of BidRx and a Ph.D. in pharmacy, said, "If you (the employee) shop wisely, you can always buy your drugs for zero."

Pharmacy benefit management systems that offer incentives for generic substitutions and disincentives for high-priced brand drugs generally work well. They often have three tiers for generics, low-price drugs, and high-price drugs. Copays are set highest for the high-price brands.

All that intelligent management notwithstanding, companies are having a very tough time managing specialty drugs that are infused or injected. The costs of those drugs are astronomical, running into the thousands each month. Yet they often work where nothing else does.

No one has found an effective way to tame the charges for specialty drugs, though some savings can be gained by going to infusion centers or self-injecting instead of receiving them at a doctor's office.

Smart purchasers also use a "step system," in which employees are asked to try lower-price alternatives before moving step by step to more expensive, still-patented pharmaceuticals.

Dental plans use a similar three-tier pricing model, in which employees enjoy big discounts for dentists in a lower-price network, lesser discounts for less competitive dentists, and no discounts out of network.

GREAT KNEE—GUARANTEED!

As an added value, a growing number of hospitals are offering warranties on top of the bundled prices if there is a readmission to fix a surgery gone badly. The practice of warranties for health care emerged in 2006, when the Geisinger Health System in Pennsylvania, through its ProvenCare program, provided coronary heart bypasses to employers and their members at a fixed, all-in rate along with a warranty against readmits. Geisinger reworked its standard procedures to make sure its outcomes improved so it didn't lose money by taking on that risk.

It has since expanded ProvenCare to angioplasty, bariatric surgery, perinatal care, and chronic conditions.

If a surgery center is willing to offer warranties, it has to be very good at what it does. There can be little variation in its quality outcomes. It has to be confident that it can limit or even eliminate costly "redos."

In any other industrial sector, such warranties are the norm. If Serigraph makes a batch of bad parts, there is no way we can charge for the replacement parts. In fact, we might have to pay some kind of penalty for having delivered the bad part in the first place.

If we were guilty of a pattern of delivering defective parts, our customer would shift new programs elsewhere. It might even yank an existing program. Now those simple realities of commerce are starting to apply in medicine. That's the marketplace kicking in.

RETAINERS FOR MEDICAL PRACTITIONERS AND OTHER DEVIATIONS FROM THE NORM

Yet another payment reform is moving rapidly across the country. Employers pay a retainer to contracted doctors and nurses for primary care. They are paid a set amount each month per member, so they cease to be worried about pumping up volumes of procedures as promoted by CPT codes.

That is called a capitated plan, in this case for primary care only. Every hospital has some capitated business, but many are considering such a fixed annual fee for the full gamut of medical care. In effect, they assume the risk for the "total cost of care."

Employers may welcome such capitated plans if the annual fee per employee is right, say $8,000 to $10,000 per year for all medical treatments and drugs.

The hospital companies would have to manage expertly to absorb the risk of costs that exceed the annual charge. Some are weighing whether to assume that risk or part of that risk.

If they did, employers would have the predictability of a preset overall health cost for a given year.

Still another reform is the simplest of them all: straight cash payments. The rapidly growing pool of consumers with high deductibles will be looking for best buys, and some convenience clinics and other providers are offering low, fixed prices for cash payments.

ACROSS THE COUNTRY, the payer revolt is bringing a variety of pricing disciplines to hammer out some order to replace the inexplicable systems of medical pricing. No one reform has yet taken over, but there are many promising innovations racing forward across the land.

Expect to see more clarity and discipline in medical pricing as managers in private companies assert themselves. They will have a much bigger impact than the endless attempts at price reform inside the industry or top-down from government payers.

LESSONS LEARNED

on Restructured Pricing

☑ Set caps on bundled prices for common medical procedures.

☑ Scrap the federal government's convoluted pricing system.

☑ Adopt a tier system for drug and dental purchases.

☑ Consider capitated charges for primary care and all care.

☑ Look for lower prices in return for cash payments.

9

ON-SITE CLINICS: COMPANIES
TAKE OVER PRIMARY CARE

J OHN SHIELY, retired CEO of Briggs & Stratton, re-
called that he was exasperated with the company's
skyrocketing costs of health care after he took over
the CEO job in 2001. "It wasn't unusual," he said, "to see
things go up 20 percent a year."

So Shiely moved quickly to take over control of his employees' primary health care. He retrieved it from big hospital corporations and brought it in-house by installing his
company's own on-site clinic.

We'll get to the results of that in a moment, but let's look at
the background that shows why his decision was necessary.

THE DISAPPEARANCE
OF THE INDEPENDENT DOCTOR

Over several decades, in most markets across the United States, hospital corporations have amassed market power by vertically integrating the supply chain for the delivery of health care. They mounted aggressive acquisition campaigns to buy up groups of primary doctors and other medical providers, including some specialist groups, testing centers, pharmacies, and rehabilitation shops. In the name of integrated medical care, they often attained near-monopoly, duopoly, or triopoly leverage in their service areas—all the way from primary care to hospice. It could be called a nonmarketplace.

Hospital corporations have made the case that buying up primary practices improves care and cuts costs. But Medicare has found just the opposite, that vertical integration raises charges. Prices more than double when services are moved from an independent doctor's office to an outpatient hospital setting.

Prices more than double when services are
moved from an independent doctor's office to an
outpatient hospital setting.

Serigraph's experience with vertical integration is similar. For example, we were buying colonoscopies for about

134

$1,200 in an independent endoscopy clinic. Six months after this small provider was acquired by a big health system, the price for a colonoscopy jumped to $1,800. Two years later, the giant system closed the clinic, removing a low-price option. This scenario had nothing to do with integrating care.

Once absorbed into the big health care systems, primary care doctors become turnstiles—directing patients to more profitable services, such as medical specialists, labs, and imaging centers. They become volume generators.

Primary care office visits in such systems commonly last only six to ten minutes. The time in the waiting room is usually much greater than the time with the doctor. Why these quick in-and-out visits? Doctors have 2,500 to 3,000 patients on their panels. They have little time for holistic, proactive care. They treat obvious symptoms and then quickly refer the patient to expensive specialists, who charge three to five times more per hour. It is what many call reactive versus proactive medicine, or "sick care" versus health care.

Because of the many handoffs in the large medical complexes, today's medicine is often quite impersonal. And despite the best efforts of big health systems at coordinated care, it is often disjointed.

An even bigger problem is overreliance on expensive specialists. It goes a long way to explaining the roiling inflation that has swelled health costs to 18 percent of America's gross domestic product—roughly double that of other developed countries where primary care is the mainstay of health care delivery.

Therein lies the frustration that executives like Shiely have experienced. "You were paying enormous amounts of money to process some pretty routine stuff," he said. "If you looked at the landscape and where you stood as a corporation, you saw your one best option was to take primary care in-house."

THE BENEFITS OF PROVIDING HEALTH CARE ON THE PREMISES

Briggs & Stratton contracted with QuadMed for its first clinic in 2002. The company made that decision after a thorough business analysis of the $800,000 needed to set up its initial clinic in Milwaukee. The payback was a quick 1.3 years.

"I don't know anybody in the company who didn't see this as a huge advantage," Shiely noted. "In fact, we used it to promote the company. And we put in a second facility at one of our large plants in Missouri because Milwaukee worked so well."

Briggs & Stratton's 7,500-square-foot clinic in Milwaukee features a busy fitness and physical therapy center. The on-site physical therapy center cuts down on lost time from factory aches and pains.

"The clinic is just part of our culture here," noted Jeff Mahlock, vice president of human relations at Briggs & Stratton.

Mahlock said that its health plan scores highly with employees and that there has been virtually no negative feedback from either union or nonunion workers. Here's a typical comment from an employee survey: "The professionalism, gentleness, as well as being attentive to my needs, has been the best I have ever received. I have been at this clinic since [the beginning] and have never received anything less than excellent medical care and concern for my well-being. My husband is leaving [the company], and I believe I will never find a medical staff that is better than this one. I deeply regret leaving."

In fiscal year 2013, Briggs & Stratton brought in its total health costs, including drugs and dental coverage, at a total of $8,868 per employee, a very competitive number. That's about 60 percent of the national average.

In a similar vein, Quad/Graphics, a major printing company, created its own QuadMed primary care operation in 1990 with one full-time clinic at its plant in Sussex, Wisconsin.

Its original purpose was to provide a great benefit to attract and retain talented employees. As the late Quad/Graphics founder Harry Quadracci memorably put it: "We'll keep you well, and, by the way, if you get sick, we'll take care of that, too."

"We'll keep you well, and, by the way, if you get sick, we'll take care of that, too."
—Harry Quadracci, Quad/Graphics founder

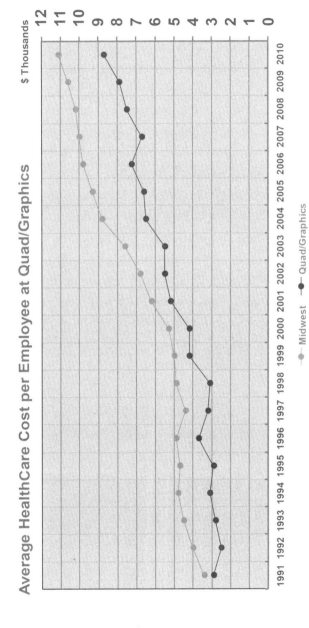

Quad/Graphics Bends the Curve

Average HealthCare Cost per Employee at Quad/Graphics

$ Thousands

Midwest   Quad/Graphics

QuadMed's Impact on Utilization in One Market

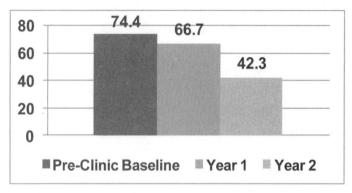

Utilization (Admits/1000)

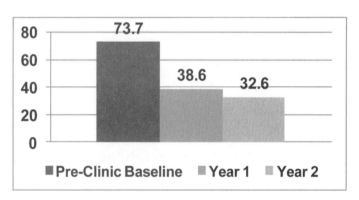

Utilization (ER Visits/100)

In 2008, though, QuadMed hired Mercer, a national benefits consulting firm, to see how the cost/benefit trade-off was working. Mercer's findings were revealing. Quad was bringing in health care at 31 percent below the Midwest average. At $7,575 per employee, Quad's health care costs were about $2,500 below average—just from proactive care. Quad wasn't using consumer-driven incentives. Note: it had average costs before taking care in-house.

Following Briggs & Stratton in Wisconsin with contracts for QuadMed on-site clinics were MillerCoors, Kohler, Northwestern Mutual Life with two, Greenheck Fan and Rockwell Automation.

By the end of 2013, QuadMed was running more than 40 clinics in 18 states for major employers like Safeway, Domtar Corp., Stihl, and Shaw Industries. It was still growing fast.

COMPANIES ALL SIZES TRY WORKSITE CLINICS

As workplace health clinics go, Walgreens is the granddaddy of them all. The Deerfield, Illinois–based pharmacy giant launched its first worksite clinics more than 40 years ago. Now Walgreens, through its affiliate Take Care Health Systems, runs more than 370 such clinics across the United States—enough to bill itself as "the leading provider of worksite health care in the country."

Among its more notable clients: Microsoft, Qualcomm, Walt Disney Co., United Airlines, BMW Manufacturing, and Sprint.

Walgreens maintains that its worksite clinics are a proven way to reduce costs and increase worker productivity by minimizing health-related absences, mainly through preventive care and chronic disease management. The rate of return on worksite health centers? It's $5.82 for every $1 invested—nearly a six-fold payback—according to Walgreens, which cites 2010 research by the American Institute for Preventive Medicine Wellness.

Sprint has reported savings of more than $1 million annually by having some of its 23,000 employees and dependents use its on-site health care center in Overland Park, Kansas. The center provides primary and acute care services, plus radiology and occupational health services.

A raft of primary care providers is entering the market of serving large corporations. For instance, Humana, a large insurer, bought Concentra to get into primary care, including worksite clinics. Concentra has about a thousand primary care doctors at more than 300 clinics. It serves employers like HP and Whole Foods Markets.

The New York Times has reported that one-quarter of the top 1,000 U.S. corporations had taken back the front end of the health care supply chain.

In one dimension, health care is a supply chain, and smart payers are starting to regard it that way. By taking back primary care, they are, in effect, disintegrating the vertically integrated supply chain of the big hospital corporations. They are dumping the "do more, bill more" model that characterizes the broken health care model.

In one dimension, health care is a supply chain, and smart payers are starting to regard it that way. By taking back primary care, they are, in effect, disintegrating the vertically integrated supply chain of the big hospital corporations.

Mid-size companies are also jumping to the on-site business model. If they are short of the 800 to 1,000 employees that Quad considers necessary for a full-time clinic, they use part-time clinics with nurses, nurse practitioners, and concierge doctors on site.

RISE OF URGENT CARE FACILITIES

Bellin Health, a large health care provider in northeast Wisconsin, has become a major innovator in the delivery of convenient and cost-effective primary care. It partnered five years ago with Shopko, a Green Bay-based department store chain, to create 50 FastCare clinics around the country. There are an estimated 1,400 such convenient or urgent-care clinics in the country, and their growth is explosive. But they are not holistic like the on-site or "near-site" clinics that serve a company's workforce.

Bellin talked to its employer customers and learned it needed to go deeper into the clinic movement to stay ahead of a fast-moving marketplace.

So Bellin has partnered with private corporations to create more than 60 on-site clinics for employees and families of those payers. Those are customized to the needs of the individual corporations.

The on-site clinics can deliver even more than primary, preventive, and urgent care. They also can handle occupational health, such as on-site accidents, employment screening, and ongoing testing needs.

George Kerwin, CEO, said Bellin started with nurse practitioners and physician assistants in the new clinics. "Within six months, we knew this was absolutely dynamic."

He views the workplace clinics as extensions of the primary care offered in his larger health system. Clearly, he is ahead of the curve in protecting the front end of his business. Some other health systems are following suit.

Employers looking at on-site care need to understand the difference between clinics owned by big-care systems and those that are independent of them. Both are an improvement over the current, fragmented model of care. But those who see the provider clinics as feeders for upscale tests, specialists, and treatments will want to contract for an independent on-site provider.

Fuld & Co., a Cambridge, Mass., corporate research and consulting firm, estimated in 2009 that workplace health clinics were saving its clients 10 percent to 30 percent on health expenses. At the time, about 2,200 such clinics existed across the country, serving 1,200 companies.

Not only do on-site clinics eliminate middleman expenses, Fuld researchers found, but they also lower the rates of both absenteeism and "presenteeism," the latter a term describing low productivity of ailing people who drag themselves through the workday.

A nurse practitioner or physician's assistant staffs the typical small-employer workplace clinic, while large-company clinics often employ doctors. Some on-site clinics include acupuncturists and dentists, pharmacy, vision care, rehabilitation services, and labs. With a critical mass of enough employees and dependents, some companies even provide cardiology, dermatology, obstetrics, gynecology, and orthopedic surgery.

ModernMed, a Phoenix-based concierge doctor franchiser, jumped into the worksite market in 2010. It cuts deals with mid-size companies (250 to 1,000 employees) to provide part-time concierge doctors. These doctors are often ones who have been frustrated with the status quo and want out of the impersonal care offered by the big systems. ModernMed pays the doctors a base salary and a bonus for good outcomes, so the high-volume mentality disappears. Its doctors see a big bump in compensation.

ModernMed charges employers an annual fee per life, what is known as a capitated plan. It can also be called a retainer. That means a set amount every year, so there is no incentive to pump volumes of procedures through their shops. In 2011 ModernMed was acquired by DaVita, a nationwide dialysis provider, and renamed Paladina Health, so its growth will accelerate with more capital.

ModernMed's founder, Dr. Jami Doucette, said, "Self-insured employers have an opportunity to create the health care system they want by controlling their health care supply chain."

"Self-insured employers have an opportunity to create the health care system they want by controlling their health care supply chain."
—DR. JAMI DOUCETTE

Paladina serves a variety of customers, like the Milwaukee Brewers and students at Wisconsin Lutheran College.

The demand for that kind of worksite primary care will intensify as ObamaCare adds millions of people into the insured ranks. The large influx will make primary care doctors a scarce commodity. They are already in short supply, so companies with their own doctors will have an advantage in recruiting and retaining employees.

Essentially, the on-site primary care turns the existing business model upside down. Instead of the specialist at the center of medical action, the primary care doctor becomes the quarterback—just like he or she was in the family-doctor era a couple generations ago.

"I've heard people describe it as a bit of a time warp. You get to go back 30, 40, 50 years and remove the insurance hassles from your practice and have this practice of 600 patients or so that you handle," said Tom Blue, executive director of the American Academy of Private Physicians, a professional association for direct-pay physicians.

As this disruptive business model races into play, two powerful levers are at work:

- The employer is back in charge of the economic side of medicine with its contracted doctor as the gatekeeper to the health care system.
- On-site providers can proactively attack the source of 80 percent of the nation's high health costs, namely chronic diseases such as diabetes, hypertension, asthma, and obesity.

It is the employer's doctor, not the big system's captive doctor, who controls key medical spending decisions.

- The company doctor orders tests and screenings at the best prices and quality ($525 for an MRI, for example, versus several thousand dollars at the scan shop of a health care conglomerate).
- The company doctor orders up the specialists, but only when warranted by patient condition—not as routine protocol.
- The company doctor or nurse practitioner orders prescriptions, with generics as the first option.

■ The company doctor orders, in collaboration with employees, admissions to hospitals or outpatient clinics.

In short, the on-site team helps immensely with proper utilization. Jim Sheeran, benefits director at MillerCoors, cited an example. "We had people so used to getting antibiotics prescribed every time they had bronchitis that they didn't like it when QuadMed doctors said, 'Let's hold off for a few days; it might not be an infection.' It took some educating—antibiotics are for bacterial infections, not viruses—but we don't have any of those kinds of issues anymore."

Dr. Mark Niedfeldt of Paladina said he went through the 2012–13 flu season without prescribing a single antibiotic. But he had to convince his patients that if they had a virus that antibiotics don't help.

He had to convince his patients that if they had a virus that antibiotics don't help.

This new primary care–based structure doesn't negate the need for a wraparound network of medical providers who provide treatment beyond primary care. But the on-site team—typically a doctor, nurse practitioner, or physician's assistant, plus nurse coaches and a dietician—can handle many nonacute conditions.

That is especially true as more analytical tools come online to help primary care teams with diagnoses. They have tons of recent information at their fingertips through software offerings like UpToDate, which updates best practices quarterly.

Most on-site company health clinics are equipped with electronic medical records (EMR). That means patients have access to their own electronic health records (EHR), and the company's health team has full information on patient status.

The on-site teams stress a collaborative, trusting relationship between themselves and an employee's family. Spouses and children generally have access to the on-site clinics. The philosophy is that medical care starts with a relationship.

Put another way, these on-site clinics are patient centric, a striking contrast to the doctor-centric model that prevails today.

In short, the employer and its on-site team offer proactive, intimate, convenient, cost-effective, integrated care in what is called "a medical home." The primary care doctor could be seen as the CEO of the medical home.

ON-SITE CLINICS A WIN-WIN FOR EMPLOYERS AND EMPLOYEES

Financially, the savings can be huge for employees.

For instance, for an on-site office visit, QuadMed charges employees only $7—much cheaper than a typical copay.

And there's no confusing Explanation of Benefits form nor additional hospital bill that comes in the mail afterward. Many companies make a wide variety of prevention and wellness programs free, and some offer free preventive procedures as well, even colonoscopies.

Employers using on-site doctors often make on-site primary care free, too. The per-life annual charge by Paladina, less than $2,000, is roughly the same as companies pay to primary doctors in the big systems under their health care plans. So converting to the on-site doctor is at worst a wash in cash outlay.

But look at all the various advantages on-site doctors deliver:

- On-site availability all week, or at least part of the week, with online scheduling
- 24/7 availability by phone or email, which big-system doctors avoid because their reimbursement is zero to minimal for such communication. Two-thirds of the on-site doctor-patient interactions can be handled by phone or email
- House calls when warranted
- Annual executive-level physicals
- Electronic health records
- 30- to 60-minute office visits, feasible because patient loads for concierge doctors typically don't exceed 600, one-fifth of the load in a typical big system
- Pre-disease recognition and risk mitigation

- Holistic oversight of all care for an employee and his or her family
- Full range of health education programs

What's not to like? One on-site doctor never sees shingles patients. He just has them send a digital photo to confirm the condition and then orders a prescription.

Think about the attractiveness of the on-site benefit to employers. Let's say an employer is trying to recruit a badly needed engineer, who would need to uproot the family and move to a new town. How good are the schools? Are good houses affordable and available? Those are often the first questions beyond the job issues. But there may be another impediment to relocation: finding a family doctor, especially after 2014.

"Not a problem," says the recruiter. "The company has its own doctors and nurses on site, and the services are free to the whole family. Plus, we have a wraparound network of high-value specialists should you need them."

The recruiter's kicker: "Talk to some of our employees. They love our health plan."

The candidate is tipped toward saying, "Offer accepted."

At Serigraph, we have cut hospital admissions in half with the new business model that revolves around on-site care. The potential savings on hospitalizations are enormous.

From a 10-year claims dig, we learned that our company was at about the national average for annual in-patient admissions—namely 71 hospitalizations per 1,000 covered

"MEDICAL HOMES" ALLOW FOR FOCUS ON RELATIONSHIP WITH THE PATIENTS

One godfather of proactive care in the format of what's known as "patient-centered medical home" is Dr. Paul Grundy. He is a national champion for integrated care that is grounded in a "whole person relationship." He urges doctors to get the relationship established first and then treat.

Why is Grundy's vision of transforming U.S. medicine to proactive primary care important?

One, because he's right.

Two, because he buys health care for IBM, which is in the top five in the United States for employment. IBM has about a half million employees and more than a million lives on its plan.

Grundy's IBM title is Global Director of Healthcare Transformation. He has a lot of clout with health insurers and providers, and he is passionate about the need to transform the old model of care.

IBM doesn't use on-site centers, preferring to prod health insurers and health systems and their community clinics to provide medical homes. (Both are IBM customers for computers.)

He asks the health plans and providers: "What will happen to you if you produce a product that we don't want to buy anymore and that we can't afford?"

He insists that IBM's providers set up medical homes that treat the whole person, not just the symptom of the day.

Payment is aligned to that vision. In medical homes, doctors aren't paid by procedure. They receive a set amount per member each month (a retainer) and bonuses for good health outcomes. In addition, he asks the primary doctors to "put barbed wire" around unnecessary services.

His approach is impacting cost trends, Grundy said, "We're pretty close to zero [increases] over 10 years."

lives from 2000 through 2007. Then, after we instituted our new health care model, admissions started to drop. They dropped to 34 hospitalizations per 1,000 covered persons in 2010. Our ratio was 41 in 2011 and 36 in 2012.

Industry insiders concede that inpatient admissions are in free fall.

Gene Miller, an executive at Paladina, believes strongly that proactive primary care can cut hospital admissions by 30 percent. Other employers report similar drops in admissions for both in-patient and outpatient cases.

The sticker price for an average hospital admission is about $24,000, so the savings climb fast.

The cumulative pattern of improving results surfaced in a five-year analysis by WeCare TLC, an on-site care vendor, at four of its workplace clinics. Said Brian Klemmer, its development director, "Establishing a clinic has often precipitated rapid increases in diagnostics, the identification of at-risk conditions, specialty visits, and drugs among patients who previously had health care coverage but poor access to health care.

"So we have learned that it may take a year, give or take, to turn a group's health care cost dynamics around. But we have achieved that consistently."

ON-SITE CLINICS constitute a major platform in the new business model for health care in America. Every American deserves one. The medical home model turns the broken, upside-down model upright. The patient/employee and primary care doctor both go back to the center stage of health care in the country.

Production-centered medicine is giving way to patient-centered health care. This disruptive breakout in the payer revolt is accelerating.

LESSONS LEARNED
on On-Site Clinics

☑ Take control of the supply chain for health care with on-site health team.

☑ Proactive primary care can greatly improve workforce health and sharply reduce costs.

☑ Equip your on-site medical home with electronic medical records, including an employee health record.

☑ Rigorous, face-to-face chronic disease management becomes possible with an on-site health team.

☑ Make primary care inexpensive or free. The payback is huge, including a drop in hospital admissions.

10

CHRONIC DISEASES: COMPANIES GO WHERE THE MONEY GOES

S AFEWAY INC., the giant grocery retailer, has embraced intensive management of chronic diseases as a key part of a broad strategic initiative that has flattened its health costs for more than 18,000 employees.

Safeway described its health cost trend as "flatlined." In 2013, it got more specific, saying its total costs inflated only 2.2 percent annually from 2005 to 2011. Its 2012 increase was about 1 percent. In medical parlance, flatlining is not a good thing. A heart has stopped beating. But in economic terms, especially in an era of out-of-control health costs, flatlining when it comes to health care costs is a very good thing. It is also a rare piece of management.

Safeway's CEO kicked off its health care campaign in 2005, and the company immediately started to see dramatic results. Five years later, it was saving almost $50 million on an annual basis. That's real money, and so far it has tackled the issue only with its nonunion employees. More savings will be realized as Safeway persuades its unions to go with its transformational plan.

Its strategy is broad-based, but the heart of its revolutionary approach is to get its people engaged as responsible adults in becoming healthier. Its managers have learned that you can't manage health costs if you don't manage health.

"We are improving the health of our people," said Kent Bradley, chief medical officer of Safeway.

"We are improving the health of our people."
—KENT BRADLEY, CHIEF MEDICAL OFFICER, SAFEWAY

That doesn't seem like a very profound discovery, but that simple truth will produce profound outcomes for individuals, organizations, and, if rolled out broadly, for the country.

First, Safeway dug out the numbers. A smoker costs $1,800 more in average annual health costs than a nonsmoker. For an obese person, it's $1,400 more. Hypertension, lack of

Safeway vs. National Health Care Cost Trend

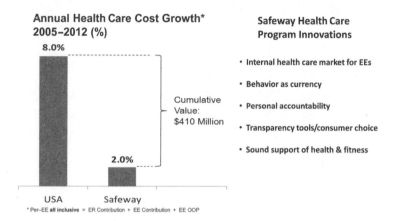

Annual Health Care Cost Growth*
2005–2012 (%)

8.0%

2.0%

USA   Safeway

* Per–EE **all inclusive** = ER Contribution + EE Contribution + EE OOP

Cumulative
Value:
$410 Million

Safeway Health Care
Program Innovations

• Internal health care market for EEs

• Behavior as currency

• Personal accountability

• Transparency tools/consumer choice

• Sound support of health & fitness

exercise, and uncontrolled cholesterol each jack up the costs by $500 to $650.

And, one-third to one-half of people with these basic chronic conditions don't adhere to their proscribed regimens. The nation's reactive health delivery system knows full well about the need to get these people back into control, but it never gets to proactive management in a serious way.

It's all about management, management, management. That's the missing link.

Safeway has become famous for just that. It has installed targeted programs and incentives to get its employees and their families to adopt healthy behaviors. Safeway hones in on five conditions: tobacco usage, healthy weight, blood pressure, blood sugar control, and cholesterol. If an individual passes metrics tests in those five areas, he or she wins a premium reduction of $1,040. For a family in compliance, it's a $2,080 reduction. Progress toward goals also earns premium rebates. The good news is that progress can be made within a few short years: From 2008 to 2012, Safeway sharply reduced the number of unhealthy people in its organization: those with hypertension by 51 percent, high glucose by 38 percent, high cholesterol by 63 percent, obesity by 20 percent, and tobacco users by 37 percent.

Clearly, given the results, the incentives do help to drive behavior.

Safeway's outcomes have caught the attention of other large corporations, so much so that the grocer started a new subsidiary, Safeway Health, to provide innovative health solutions and change management consulting services.

MANAGEMENT TECHNIQUES MEET INDIVIDUAL RESPONSIBILITY

For companies familiar with Six Sigma quality disciplines, it should come as no surprise that rigorous management can work in the field of health care, just as it works in managing processes in a factory.

For example, I have asked the managers at Serigraph to get all of our diabetics—100 percent of them—under control. In Six Sigma terminology, a breakdown in a process results in a defect—in this case, a diabetic who is out of control. We have set a goal for our health team and

IMPACT OF DISEASE MANAGEMENT
WITH DRUG REGIMEN ADHERENCE

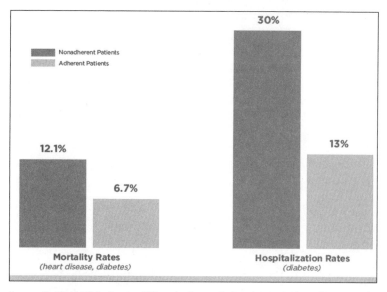

Source: Castlight White Paper—"What the Doctor Ordered: Prescription Adherence with Transparency." Reprinted with permission.

employees of zero defects—no diabetics out of control for the three relevant blood tests. And the goal is in sight.

Companies like Briggs & Stratton and Quad/Graphics mentioned earlier provide educational programs, incentives, and regular testing. Quad/Graphics gives insulin free to diabetics who have successfully managed their disease.

So does Briggs & Stratton, where 70 percent to 80 percent of its diabetics are in its management program for that condition. Briggs has done the hard numbers, and it shows a $3.50 return for every $1 invested in the program.

ENCOURAGING HEALTH IN THE OFFICE

Many other companies have joined the march toward wellness, all based on the generally accepted analysis that 80 percent of the nation's health costs are caused by 20 percent of the people, those with one of the 15 chronic diseases. Few debate the broad 80/20 concept, evidenced by the fact that more than half of U.S. companies offer some kind of wellness program.

Managers are supposed to be able to sort things out. If 80 percent of costs were on the chronic disease side of the problem, what professional manager would fail to deal with employee health as the major thrust of managing health care costs?

Yet, in the past, most prevention and wellness programs were anemic at best. They offered brochures, passive websites, and a few pieces of uncollected policy, like subsidized health club memberships. They contact people by telephone, a method that produces limited results at best.

With health and health costs becoming a strategic imperative, corporate executives are getting a lot more hardnosed about positive health results. They are installing aggressive programs that center on face-to-face interactions between employees and medical teams.

The third-largest private employer in South Carolina, J M Smith Corp., a wholesale drug distributor and health care IT company, got serious about its employees' health in 2004 and has ratcheted up its programs every year.

To get a handle on individual and population health, it requires an annual health risk assessment, including a blood draw, at its on-site clinic. People identified with a chronic disease are offered an individualized care program. The company offers various incentives, such as a $500 bonus if a weight goal is met in six months and another $3,000 if the weight is kept off for two years.

Rhonda Lockhart, corporate HR director, said the company has learned that people with chronic conditions cost twice as much as well people, but, happily, those who join a disease management program can bring their costs down to average levels. And they can do it in relatively short order.

Last year, J M Smith's costs were $11,786 per unwell employee versus $5,800 for well employees. To get to wellness, Lockhart believes in "a service model" with the employee as the customer.

One of the early movers in recognizing that workforce health is a strategic issue was Jim Hagedorn, a former F-16 pilot who served as CEO of Scotts Miracle-Gro starting in 2005. As a way to tackle soaring health costs, he inaugurated a smoking ban, free smoking cessation programs, free doctor care for 8,000 employees and their families, exhaustive health risk assessments and health coaches in an on-site medical and fitness center, and free generic drugs.

According to a 2007 Bloomberg article, he is famous for having said, "My view is we choose not to employ smokers because it comes right down to us saying that as a culture we care about our people and we are not going to tolerate suicidal behavior."

"We care about our people and we are not going to tolerate suicidal behavior."

His was an "in-your-face" approach that used carrots and sticks to change employee behaviors and cut chronic diseases. He questioned why other American employers weren't attacking wellness issues like obesity and smoking.

Despite worries about coming off as a "Big Brother" company, most employees don't see aggressive health programs as intrusive. Rather, they see a company that is investing in their health. That's a positive moral factor, much like tuition reimbursement for education is seen as a positive investment in an employee's value.

Jeffrey Mahloch, the vice president of human resources at Briggs & Stratton who led its early move to on-site medical care, said its health plan is the most favorite aspect of the company in the eyes of its 2,000 Milwaukee employees. Proactive health care "is just part of our culture here," he said.

HEALTH RISK ASSESSMENTS

A common denominator at companies leading the way to a new business model for the delivery of health care is the health risk assessment. Some companies are making the mini-physical mandatory. Others offer big incentives to encourage the annual checkup.

A major advantage of mandatory assessments for employees and spouses (not children, as they are generally inexpensive for a health plan) is that managers get an aggregate read on the health of the workforce.

The on-site medical teams, who often deliver the assessments and build personal relationships with employees in the process, see the personal medical information so they can intervene on an individual basis. They intervene immediately when a high-risk situation is uncovered.

On top of that, though, managers gain valuable workforce information, such as average cholesterol, percentage of smokers, average body mass index (BMI), and numbers of diabetics. Red flags go off with bad readings of workforce health. Corrective programs can be brought to bear. That's how closed-loop management systems are supposed to work.

For instance, the Serigraph dashboard for the health of its co-workers showed generally positive results, but also some red flags.

From 2011 to 2012, we reduced our high-cholesterol count from 82 people to 61. Great!

But we didn't move the needle on BMI. In fact, it went the wrong way from 2005 to 2012. In a common cohort group of 364 employees, we went from 102 with high-risk body mass to 122. Our co-workers are 17 pounds overweight on average. Obesity is our biggest health issue, with an obvious price tag attached.

So we have reengineered our weight-loss programs, and they appear to be working. We slightly reduced our high-risk BMI people from 2011 to 2012. But, it's clear we have more innovative work to do in dealing with our small part of the national obesity epidemic.

Overall, though, in all categories, we dropped our high-risk population from 22 percent in 2005 to 16 percent in 2012.

CEOs MUST LEAD THE WAY IN MENTAL HEALTH TOO

Systematic management of chronic conditions generally doesn't happen in the current reactive U.S. model. Don't CEOs have a patriotic duty to lead the way to a better model?

There is plenty of innovative work to do. For instance, if face-to-face treatment works on-site for physical illnesses, why would that model not work for mental illnesses?

So, a new frontier for proactive primary care is mental health. Levels of mental illness can be elicited in the annual assessment process through a simple, proven eight-question screen, called the PHQ-9.

Major depression, for example, which affects about 7 percent of the population, can be detected through the PHQ-9. Once it is detected, it can be treated.

There are also effective screens for addictive behaviors.

Company managers have to set the stage for mental and behavioral health initiatives. They have to reiterate loud and clear that all health issues, including mental health, are privacy protected. And they need to launch educational programs to remove any stigma attached to seeking help for such illnesses as anxiety, depression, and addiction.

Companies often offer Employee Assistance Programs (EAPs) to deal with such issues, but only a small percentage of employees go there. At Serigraph, it's about 2 percent. So, adding behavioral treatment professionals to the on-site teams will be the next step. A few companies already bring EAP help on-site.

Dr. Richard Brown of the University of Wisconsin–Madison has worked his entire career to improve primary care in terms of behavior change. "Until primary care does this better, it makes perfect sense for employers to deal with behavioral issues through on-site health teams."

He adds that many primary care providers conduct behavioral screenings, "but none deliver recommended interventions because their physicians and nurses simply don't have time."

Why not fix that gap at employer clinics? Untreated, depressed people are obviously not the most productive or creative employees.

Our first PHQ-9 screen at Serigraph identified three people with high-risk depression and nine others with major issues. Our health coaches are working with those 12 people.

Our on-site health coach also uses a new technique called motivational interviewing to get after risky drinking and smoking reduction—two behaviors that cost companies major dollars.

Brown's company, Wellsys, has quantified the savings from using behavioral screening and intervention for smoking, depression, and binge drinking. He calculates the possible savings in year one at $895 per employee across a workforce, with more savings building up in following years.

ComPsych Corp., a leading EAP provider, has pointed the way to more savings by dealing with workplace stress and anxiety. Its 2013 analysis found that one-third of employees across all industries and occupations report feeling tense or anxious much of the time. ComPsych said employees with full-blown anxiety disorders are three to five times more likely to go to a doctor, with symptoms that mimic physical illness.

Brown and others have learned an important lesson about cost effectiveness. Health coaches don't have to be highly educated medical professionals. Less expensive college graduates can be trained relatively quickly to deal with behavioral issues.

Conclusion? It's time to address that illness on site.

FROM A STRATEGIC MANAGEMENT PERSPECTIVE, chronic disease management represents an enormous opportunity to reverse the long trend toward worse health in the United States and uncontrolled inflation in health care. The drop in the nation's percentage of smokers from a high of 40 percent two decades ago to today's 19 percent proves it can be done. The goal should be zero. Expect businesses to move fast to capitalize on the opportunities from basic behavior change.

Going one step further, the argument can be made that highly trained medical professionals ought to deal only with treatments and interventions, what can be called "sick care." That would delegate to employers the challenge of managing their populations to better health, what accurately could be called "health care." After all, we employers are the ones with a long-term relationship with our people and a financial stake in their health and well-being.

LESSONS LEARNED
from Chronic Disease Management

☑ You can't manage health costs without managing health.

☑ Employers are uniquely positioned to affect the health of their workforces.

☑ Six Sigma disciplines can be brought to bear on the process of managing chronic diseases, just like any other process.

☑ Incentives, wisely designed, can stimulate better employee behaviors and treatment regimens.

☑ Mandatory mini-physicals enable tracking metrics on a health care dashboard.

☑ An on-site clinic can be effective for behavioral screening and intervention, including mental illnesses.

11

HEALTH AS ASSET: COMPANIES COME TO NEW UNDERSTANDING

PATRICK CUNNINGHAM is a leading voice for helping Americans understand that good health is an asset—not just a physical asset but also a financial asset. As chief executive of Manning & Napier, a major benefits management company and consultant based in Rochester, New York, Cunningham counsels his many business customers to treat employee health as a valuable resource for both employer and employee.

Cunningham was one of the first to see a health-wealth convergence in the management of health investments and retirement financial assets, such as 401(k) plans.

169

It's one of those ideas that seems patently obvious, once someone like Cunningham articulates it. Think of how many ways he is right:

- As personal health accounts build up—the average funded account now holds a balance of several thousand dollars and some have hit six figures—they can be managed side by side with the other pieces of an employee's retirement portfolio. That allows the allocations in the two accounts to be coordinated for the right mix of stocks and bonds and other securities. In this dimension, health literally is a financial asset.

- The Health Savings Accounts (HSAs) and Health Reimbursement Accounts (HRAs) of healthy employees have fewer drawdowns and build faster than those of unhealthy people.

- If employees stay healthy, they miss fewer days of work, and, if paid hourly, fewer days of pay.

- In some organizations, employees can accumulate unused sick days and cash them in at retirement.

- Healthy people are more productive, which should mean faster job advancement.

- Healthy people often enjoy better morale, which helps job performance and, therefore, leads to raises.

- A healthy retired couple will spend as much as a quarter of a million dollars less in their post-work years than an unhealthy couple.

- Poor health leads to higher medical bills, therefore financial stress, which, in turn, causes health issues.
- An unhealthy employee, whose savings have been drained by high health costs, will have to work later in life. It's reality that health care for older people costs twice that for workers in their prime.
- "Financial wellness" reduces stress, which, in turn, reduces physical and mental illnesses.

The combined impact of those positive monetary outcomes from good health has led innovative companies to more rigorous health planning at both the corporate and personal levels.

FINANCIAL AND HEALTH DASHBOARDS

At the corporate level, enlightened companies have installed two dashboards to track their health assets. They use a monthly financial dashboard to measure every element of their health care expenses. That's just rigorous management. But they also use a health dashboard to track improvements in overall workforce health.

The financial dashboard looks monthly at line items like hospital costs, doctor expenses, dental, drugs, workers' compensation, and HSA or HRA contributions. It tracks total costs and employer and employee share, compared to the previous year, to budget, and to national and regional norms. It also breaks down the costs per employee and per life.

The cost profile has to be pulled from several sources to get the full picture, but it has to be done. As everyone knows, you can't manage without real, timely, and accurate numbers.

The health dashboard is generated on an annual basis. It tracks metrics like average cholesterol across the workforce, blood pressure, body mass, numbers of diabetics and percentage under control, other chronic disease numbers, hospital admits, ER visits, and absenteeism.

The health dashboard ... tracks metrics like average cholesterol across the workforce, blood pressure, body mass, numbers of diabetics and percentage under control, other chronic disease numbers, hospital admits, ER visits, and absenteeism.

These two dashboards enable clear analysis and sharp managerial decisions on health care policy.

There are vendors like PlanIT that do an annual claims dig to develop the health dashboard. These analytics are invaluable. The other source of data that becomes information and analysis is the on-site health team, which can aggregate the results of individual health risk assessments into a mosaic of the overall workforce health.

INDIVIDUAL HEALTH PLANS

Many companies already do a good job of helping employees with career planning and with pension or 401(k) planning. But smart employers are now adding a third planning process—an individual health plan for each employee and spouse. All three affect long-term employee prosperity.

Many companies already do a good job of helping employees with career planning and with pension or 401(k) planning. But smart employers are now adding a third planning process—an individual health plan for each employee and spouse. All three affect long-term employee prosperity.

At Serigraph, we ask employees and spouses to sign on for an individual health plan during their annual health coaching sessions. The on-site medical team slices and dices the individual's report card based on results from the required health risk assessment with the employee or spouse, and then the person decides what to do about health deficits. Employee and health coach both sign the 12-month personal plan.

For example, for a diabetic, an individualized management program is put into play, involving diet, exercise, weight, and drug regimens. Incentives attach to the annual

EXAMPLE OF EMPLOYEE HEALTH PLAN

InHealth Risk Report™ | 2013

My Screening Profile

Name	Jane Smith
Employee ID	123456
Gender	F
Age	48
Tobacco Use	No
Height	65
Weight	148
Phone	000.000.0000
Email Y / N	

Preventive Exams & Screenings

Recommendations based on your current age and gender.
Checked boxes indicate exams needed.

- ☒ Annual Physical Exam March 2012
- ☐ Vision Exam Jan 2012
- ☐ Skin Exam March 2012
- ☒ Hearing Exam
- ☐ Pap Test March 2012
- ☐ Mammogram/Breast Exam March 2012
- ☐ Colonoscopy 2011
- ☐ Digital Rectal Exam NA
- ☐ PSA Test NA
- ☐ Dental Check Jan 2013

My Biometric Summary

Biometric Tested	Result	Recommended Range
Percent Body Fat	30%	Females <28%; Males <22%
Body Mass Index (BMI)	23.1	18.5 - 24.9
Waist Circumference		Females 18-35; Males 16-40 inches
Blood Pressure	100/64	Systolic <120 / Diastolic <80 is optimal.
Total Cholesterol	173	TC < 200mg/dL is desirable.
Triglycerides	136	TRG <150 mg/dL is optimal.
HDL ("Good Cholesterol")	33	Men: HDL ≥40 mg/dL AND Women: HDL ≥50 mg/dL is optimal.
LDL ("Bad Cholesterol")	113	LDL <100 mg/dL is optimal.
TC/HDL Ratio	5.3	A ratio of <3.5 is optimal.
Glucose	93	Fasting glucose <100mg/dL is desirable.

Risk Assessment

The following areas need attention.

Nutrition Habits	___
Physical Activity	X
Lung Health	___
Skin Health	___
Heart Health	X
Diabetes Awareness	___
Digestive Health	___
Emotional Health	___
Personal Safety	___
Advanced Directives	___

Plan for the Year

Main behavior change focus: ___ Physical activity ___

Recommended programs at Serigraph:

☒ Healthy Habits, Healthy Living (☐Diabetes ☐Heart Health) ☐LME Programs: ___

☐ Appointment with Chiropractor, Dietitian, Health Coach, Nurse Practitioner ___

Short-term goal: ___ 3x week 30 mins = 90 mins/wk ___

Long-term goal: ___ consistent exercise routine ___

I plan to work towards my wellness goals and consent to have the health coach reach out to me during the year.

Coach Jones	Jane Smith	3/1/13
Coach Signature	Participant Signature	Date

Confidential Information

Interra Health 1675 N Barker Rd Brookfield WI 53045

plan. Insulin, for example, is provided free to individuals in the diabetes program.

The combination of the annual assessment, health report card, goal setting, and support program become a powerful platform to get to better health. This planning process can be used in other proactive ways. Serigraph has just added education and counseling for end-of-life planning, including making available forms for Advance Directives. One-quarter of our co-workers signed up in the first go-around in 2012. The goal is 100 percent.

Gundersen Health System in La Crosse, Wisconsin, has already proved that proactivity on Advance Directives can work wonders. More than 90 percent of its Medicare patients have signed such directives.

While only a small percentage of working Americans die during any given work year, the anguish and costs surrounding end-of-life episodes can be high. Both can be mitigated by advance planning and clear communication before a person becomes terminally ill.

Employers, of course, will steer clear of advice on the content of end-of-life decisions. They neither want nor need knowledge of what goes into the directive. But they can make the planning tools and process available.

That can also help employees deal with older relatives who face such issues. Remember: Most Americans want to die at home. Their second choice is often hospice. They don't want to die in a hospital. Therefore, smart employers make hospice free. Palliative care is often a better answer than a grueling hospital stay, and it's much less expensive.

Most Americans want to die at home. Their second choice is often hospice. They don't want to die in a hospital.

ALLEVIATING STRESS

As companies elevate health to a strategic priority, they make wellness and fitness part of their cultures. Perhaps none have done as much to promote health as an asset as Promega Corp., a biotechnology company in Madison, Wisconsin. It offers a Zen Zone.

This is a place where employees can go on its environmentally friendly campus to relieve stress through classes in yoga, meditation, or Reiku therapy. The Zen Zone also includes a sauna, relaxation room, and a tranquil outdoor patio. The company subsidizes on-site massage therapy and acupuncture.

Promega is on the cutting edge of the wellness movement, but it is far from alone. Other nearby examples are Royle Printing and Sub-Zero, both also in Madison. Royle subsidizes health club memberships and offers extra vacation days for losing weight and keeping it off.

Sub-Zero, a manufacturer of cooling units, helps employees buy bicycles, and it reduces employee health plan contributions by 20 percent if they participate in wellness activities.

Bretting Manufacturing, in Ashland, Wisconsin, on the shores of Lake Superior, helps pass the long winters by offering a 40,000-square-foot health center with a basketball court, tennis courts, and a weight room. Families and customers are invited. Its on-site nurse practitioner has an office in the middle of the manufacturing floor.

Many companies now offer walking paths, on-site flu shots, along with annual biometric screenings. Promega one-ups them all with most of the above, plus a wellness center, a mothers' room, a farmers market on the campus for purchase of locally grown produce on Thursdays, a 24/7 fitness room in each of five buildings, two volleyball courts, a basketball court, and land for vegetable gardens on campus.

Bill Linton, Promega's founder, adamantly supports the wellness initiative, and that gives his human relations staff the clout it needs to get creative on the wellness front.

Has Promega gone too far? Skeptics in health care would say so. But no one can argue that Promega doesn't care about its people. That positive morale factor alone is compelling.

Companies say they see the concrete benefits. Toni Stoikes, benefits manager at Sub-Zero, said that a deep dig on claims data over the last three years shows a downward trend on catastrophic occurrences. That means fewer expensive admissions to hospitals.

HP, with 330,000 employees in 70 countries, tackles wellness on a global level.

"We as a company really care about the employees," said Elaine Beddome, vice president of corporate benefits at HP. "You've got to make wellness part of your culture."

Even though many countries where HP operates have government-run health care, paid for by indigenous taxpayers, the company still invests extra dollars in health as an asset. It's a strategic initiative, said Beddome, "not just an HR initiative."

HP's "Winning with Wellness" program homes in on physical wellness, financial well-being, and stress management. It has learned that employee financial problems can cause major stress, a health liability, and that stress raises health costs. HP is addressing the health-wealth connection.

Beddome reported that HP held its medical cost inflation to less than 2 percent from 2010 to 2012.

HARD-NOSED EXECUTIVES often question wellness programs, but they have to admit that the old laissez-faire model on health hasn't worked. Reactive fixes when an employee breaks down have failed. So smart CEOs see promotion of health as an asset as the right thing to do and as a low-risk financial bet.

The proactive, take-charge approach to care makes ever more sense as all parties come to the conclusion that good health is not only a blessing but also money in the bank for employer and employee.

It also makes sense to take the long-term view that workforce health is a strategic asset. Because it is, any way you cut it.

LESSONS LEARNED
from Health as Asset

☑ Teach executive team to view workforce health as a financial asset.

☑ Ask employees to regard their health as a blessing and a financial asset.

☑ Develop rigorous health care analytics expressed in two dashboards, one financial and one on population health.

☑ Integrate portfolio management of HSAs and 401(k)s.

☑ Ask each employee to commit to an annual health plan.

☑ Promote Advance Directives.

☑ Make workforce health a strategic priority.

12

Other Payers Join the
Marketplace Revolution

T O MOVE A PUBLIC ENTITY to innovative management of health care benefits is not for the faint
of heart. Enter Kristi Foy and Valley Elliehausen,
administrative officers for two good-size school districts
in Wisconsin that have moved into self-insurance and
consumer-driven health plans (CDHPs).

They are in the vanguard, but a growing number of other
public payers are moving to adopt the pragmatic reforms
that have worked in the private sector.

Foy, a Duke-educated attorney who manages benefits
for the Elmbrook School District west of Milwaukee, took

the lead in 2011 and persuaded its teachers and staff that a CDHP could provide fiscal advantages and predictability for the district, and that the specter of hyperinflation in premiums could be contained.

The Elmbrook CDHP that she installed features a $4,000 deductible for a family offset by a $2,000 Health Reimbursement Account (HRA) or Health Savings Account (HSA). For singles, it's $2,000 and $1,000.

"We have been very pleasantly surprised," Foy said. After two years, 97 percent of the 1,150 covered employees have responded to premium incentives and have signed up for the CDHP. Feedback has been universally positive.

Elliehausen, who holds an MBA from Concordia University and is the chief operations officer for the West Bend School District north of Milwaukee, has pushed the envelope even further. The district moved to self-insurance in the 1980s, then bid out its business and saved millions by moving away from a locked-in health insurance plan run by the teachers union. From that base, Elliehausen used the freedom granted to local government under Wisconsin's notorious Act 10, which stripped bargaining over benefits from public unions, to install a CDHP in 2011. The savings mounted. By 2013, CDHP participation reached 88 percent.

Then she laid the groundwork for an on-site primary care clinic headed by a physician's assistant to serve the district's 1,100 employees. It struck a clinic contract in early 2013 with Healthstat, a North Carolina-based company, which operates more than 350 such clinics in 32 states. The new

clinic, manned by a physician's assistant, was warmly received by employees when it opened in the fall of 2013.
Big financial rewards were structured to encourage healthy
regimens.

Susan Kinzler, executive vice president of Healthstat,
said about 15 percent of its business is with public sector
employers, but that percentage is growing fast as schools
and local governments figure out that better workforce
health brings lower costs. She sees on-site clinics as disruptive to a delivery system that isn't working, but not in a
historical context. Rather, they are a return to the days in
southern towns when employers provided housing, stores,
and a company doc who made house calls.

---

*On-site clinics... are a return to the days in
southern towns when employers provided housing,
stores, and a company doc who made house calls.*

"The scary thing is why a disruptive model needs to take
place," she said. "The root cause of the inflation is the lack
of coordinated care [in the present model] to show people
how to take care of themselves."

The on-site clinics fill that gap. They become a medical
home, the pivot point for holistic care.

Elliehausen looks systemically at health care and looks
for a positive return on health investments—the concept
of investment return is largely foreign to the public sector.

She views the district's staff as its principal asset. So, she asks, why not invest in their health?

"If it's not advancing the district, why are we doing it? Employers that have on-site clinics see it as a win-win because you incent your population to want to take care of their health. Our clinic is going to work with employees on current health issues, but also will have a strong focus on preventive measures," she said.

MANAGING COSTS IN THE PUBLIC SECTOR IS A WIN-WIN

Elliehausen and Foy are leading the way, but many public sector employers are moving to better models for health benefits because they have to. The pain of skyrocketing health inflation has become unbearable. Local governments often pay more than $20,000 per employee. Compare that to the per-employee number in West Bend schools: $9,850 in 2012. At 1,100 employees, the savings compared to unmanaged plans at $20,000 is some $11 million a year.

From the savings, the district has found money for raises, for long-deferred maintenance, and put $5 million from reserves into a building program for a new middle school. That helped a $23 million referendum pass by a narrow margin.

In Wisconsin, school districts in Green Bay, Beloit, and Kenosha have also installed on-site clinics. In addition, a half-dozen districts and a half-dozen counties have put in consumer-driven plans.

"It [a consumer-driven plan] is definitely something many districts are looking at," said Robert Butler of the Wisconsin Association of School Boards.

Change management takes leadership, education, and a campaign of communication, especially in unionized units. Government leaders have to engage employees in a dialogue and explain that change can be a good thing, that innovation can add value, that the old models are unsustainable.

It can be done. But the profit motivation to cut costs is not as present in the public sector. Nor is the fear of loss and business failure. Bureaucrats keep their jobs and move ahead by keeping their heads down and not making mistakes. They are not rewarded for taking risks.

The profit motivation to cut costs is not as present in the public sector. Nor is the fear of loss and business failure. Bureaucrats keep their jobs and move ahead by keeping their heads down and not making mistakes. They are not rewarded for taking risks.

Nonetheless, there is progress. Twelve states now offer CDHP plans with HSAs or HRAs. According to Kaiser's annual employer survey, about 8 percent of public employees are in a CDHP, compared to 24 percent in the private sector.

Mitch Daniels led the nation's governors when he installed a CDHP for state employees as governor in Indiana. He moved on to head Purdue University, where he introduced the same thing.

Public employers, per Kaiser, do a better job on prevention programs, 96 percent offering at least one versus 61 percent in private companies.

Ann Boynton, who contracts for health care for 1.3 million public employees in California as a deputy executive officer of CalPERS, the biggest benefit outfit in the country, states, "We know the right things to do. We just need to get it done. There has been a huge failure of leadership.

"We are going to break the back of costs doubling every 10 years."

CalPERS is contracting with insurers and providers for high-intensity case management aimed at better health. They have reaped a 44 percent drop in inpatient hospital admissions and a 27 percent drop in outpatient visits.

WHAT ABOUT THE FEDERAL GOVERNMENT?

The federal government cannot be expected to move toward better management of costs as a payer because it is consumed with the complexity and confusion surrounding implementation of the Affordable Care Act on access and insurance reform.

Once again, recognize that insurance reform is not—repeat not—reform of the model for delivering care. The new law deals with who's covered, what's covered, and who pays for it. That's important, but it's also a detour from fixing a failed economic model. It will be years before the feds figure out they have a lot more work to do—the kind of work that's been done at the grassroots level in the private sector over the last decade.

Take Dennis Smith, for example. He headed the Medicaid program for the last Bush administration and did little to dent the cost escalation of the program. Smith then took over the Medicaid program for Gov. Scott Walker in Wisconsin. He spent his two years there worrying about who was on the Medicaid rolls and who could be taken off.

When I asked him why he didn't add some incentives and disincentives to curb the widespread overutilization by Medicaid recipients, he blew off such basic change.

Smith said it would be politically impossible to give a poor person an HSA of $3,000 along with a high deductible. His political reservations may be justified. But, if not an HSA, Mr. Smith, why not an HRA, an account in the client's name? That kind of account, which can only be drawn down for health care, could accomplish the same incentive result. That should be politically palatable to both parties at both the state and federal levels.

If accomplished, abuse of the program would be sharply curtailed. No Medicaid client would order a $1,500 ambulance ride in a nonemergency situation if the money came out of his or her personal account. They would get there in a cheaper manner and keep the unused HRA balance for future bills.

There is some movement on the Medicaid front. Indiana got a waiver from the federal government to experiment with CDHP dynamics with its Medicaid population.

Or why not Reference-Based Pricing in Medicaid like CalPERS uses to cap procedure payments? For example, Medicaid recipients would be directed to centers that offer colonoscopies for $1,500, and that would be the maximum paid by the government. Why should taxpayers pay more?

One day, such fresh thinking will prevail in the public sector, because the costs have become unsustainable.

As Smith left Madison, he left behind a bipartisan Medicaid increase that chewed up close to half of all new Wisconsin state revenues in the following two-year budget.

The Medicaid crunch is especially cruel to all parties:

- Poor people can't find doctors or dentists who will take them on because of the low government reimbursements.
- Medical providers swear they can't make money under Medicaid price controls.
- At the same time, even with low prices, state governments are staggering under the financial weight of paying their 40 percent of the tab.

There are no winners in Medicaid because the program is managed so ineptly. And it's getting worse as ObamaCare adds millions of people to the Medicaid rolls.

You have to feel for hospital CEOs and CFOs. They could suck up the low to nonexistent margins on Medicaid patients in the past by massively cost shifting to private payers.

That explains the long pattern of double-digit inflation in premiums for private payers while the overall inflation of health costs was in the high single digits. It was government price controls on one-half of the nation's health care bill and runaway prices for the other half that was paid by companies and their employees.

Now, though, hospital executives are in a new world. They are in a Medicaid vise. Their unprofitable Medicaid business is about to explode, but they can no longer shove their revenue needs off on private payers. The payer revolt means they have nowhere to go for revenue boosts.

They have no alternative but to get more lean and efficient, and most of them don't know how. Private payers are unsympathetic, having themselves faced revenue stagnation or worse. They have had to downsize, streamline, consolidate, outsource—whatever—to cut overheads and costs. The hospital corporations will just have to do the same as the revenue fairy disappears.

States that might want to move ahead on reforming Medicaid are hamstrung by their partnership with the federal government. It's roughly a 60 percent to 40 percent federal-state split of the costs, so the feds control the strings on the program. States need a federal waiver to innovate, and not many of those have been forthcoming. Result: no real change for the better.

AT THE LOCAL LEVEL, though, federal or state approval is generally not required. The innovations can happen there. That is starting to happen—not with the velocity of change in the private sector, but real change nonetheless.

So, innovation in the public sector will also start at the grassroots level, one entity after another, just like it started out in the private sector. Taxpayers can only hope and pray these efforts will expand and continue.

One of the early movers on health care reforms in the public sector was Bob Ziegelbauer, county executive for Manitowoc County in Wisconsin. Ziegelbauer, who holds an MBA from The Wharton School, started a campaign six years ago to persuade his seven unions to move to a consumer-driven structure for health care. It has worked.

"Our costs have stayed relatively flat," he said. "It's here to stay, even in the face of turbulence in our world politically and economically."

Every year he adds features, such as his new Spin Program, which uses incentives and disincentives to guide employees to providers that offer high quality and low prices for elective procedures. That has meant a tough decision to steer away from a Manitowoc provider that scored poorly on both dimensions of value.

Ziegelbauer sees an emerging culture of consumerism that is reshaping the business model for health care in the world of government.

"The bottom-line stuff," he said, "is all positive."

He would welcome fast followers.

LESSONS LEARNED

☑ Public payers can deploy the same basic management tools that private payers are using to bend the cost curve.

☑ Public employees like consumer plans once they experience them.

☑ Government doesn't have to bear unending financial pain from bloated benefits.

13

EMPLOYEES, EMPLOYERS, NATION: WIN-WIN-WIN

THE BIGGEST WINNERS from the bottom-to-top revolution toward a disruptive new model for the delivery of health care in America are the employees of leading-edge companies.

But they are not the only winners in a reengineered health system. So are the employers and citizens of this country, whose priorities have been heretofore crowded out by medical spending run amok. If employees are lucky enough to work for a payer who makes their health and health costs a strategic priority, they are winners many times over.

How many times have you heard CEOs say, "Our people are our most valuable resource"? If they walk their talk, they should be investing in a health model that works, one that replaces the busted model that fixes people when they are broken with one that keeps people healthy up front. Reactive intervention after people become sick produces neither optimum health nor affordable financial obligations.

In short, they need to make workforce health and health costs a strategic priority.

How many times have you heard CEOs say, "Our people are our most valuable resource"? If they walk their talk, they should be investing in a health model that works, one that replaces the busted model that fixes people when they are broken with one that keeps people healthy up front.

Think of the ways that employees win with the new model that has been hammered out at the grassroots level, company by company, innovator by innovator, consumer by consumer. Here's just a partial list:

■ **Lower premiums.** Best-practice companies are able to eliminate or sharply reduce premium increases in years when they successfully tame costs.

- **Free medical services.** Leading-edge payers offer free primary care, often in convenient on-site clinics, as well as free prevention and wellness programs.
- **Free prescriptions.** Some payers make generic drugs free to employees who choose them over branded pharmaceuticals. And they cut deals to buy other drugs at best prices.
- **Chronic disease management.** Conditions like diabetes, asthma, high blood pressure, and depression are treated aggressively in smart plans, reducing long-term catastrophes.
- **Savings growth.** When employees keep themselves healthy, thus avoiding medical charges, balances in their Health Savings Accounts (HSAs) or Health Reimbursement Accounts (HRAs) grow. Some tax-advantaged HSAs are now in the five and even six figures.
- **Lower charges.** When employees take advantage of good deals for treatments, the out-of-pocket amounts for their deductibles and coinsurance are lower.
- **Procedure rebates.** Some smart payers offer incentives, such as $2,000 for a hip replacement, if the plan member takes his or her medical business to a Center of Value where quality is high and price is low. Other companies charge the employee nothing for surgeries if they will go to a Center of Value.

- **Fewer lost paydays.** The healthy employee loses fewer days of pay to illnesses and hospitalizations.
- **Richer retirement.** A healthy couple spends far less on health care in retirement years than an unhealthy couple, to the tune of a quarter-million dollars.
- **Catastrophic cap.** Employees and their families are protected from the costs of major medical situations. Most plans include a maximum out-of-pocket amount that an employee is required to pay in a given year.
- **More productive.** Healthy people do better on the job, which augurs well for promotions and compensation during a career.

As for employers, getting a handle on health and health cost inflation can be a matter of survival. Companies typically pick up three-quarters of the health care tab, so health benefits are often the second, third, or fourth biggest cost bucket for a business. That's the major reason why sharp executives have made workforce health a strategic priority.

Companies typically pick up three-quarters of the health care tab, so health benefits are often the second, third, or fourth biggest cost bucket for a business.

Matching the prices of global competitors, whether for a product or a service, requires aggressive control of costs across every line item. It's imperative in today's world to make employees partners in managing costs in general, and that has to include health costs.

EMPLOYEES AS PARTNERS IN CONTROLLING HEALTH COSTS

Beyond cost reduction, some executives have figured out that they have a competitive leg up on companies that tolerate bloated benefit costs.

John Mackey, founder of Whole Foods Market, commented about his campaign for workforce health in a Booz & Co. white paper:

"It's a win-win strategy for all stakeholders involved. When we have healthy team members, they are happier, and happy team members provide better customer service to our shoppers. It also leads to the company needing to spend less on healthcare, which is better for investors."

Surveys of employees show that they highly value the investments made by employers in the health of their families. They appreciate being treated like engaged adults in co-managing health services.

That engagement, of course, is what's missing in the top-down mandates that are the essence of the new federal law. That law deals with access and insurance reform, and it lays down a heavy dose of rules and the penalties for noncompliance.

Perhaps fatally, it does little to mitigate health cost inflation, the all-consuming issue. To not deal with the cost structure is to be peripheral or superficial. The nation's bill for the new law will end up costing at least double what its proponents purported it to cost. It's almost as if costs were irrelevant.

Further, the Affordable Care Act moves away from choice and competition. It supports "Accountable Care Organizations" (ACOs), which are combinations of big health plans and big providers. In short, it's big government promoting big health care. Yet neither insurers nor hospital companies have demonstrated the ability to control their costs.

Worse, the ACOs offer narrow networks that inherently limit choice. Consumers can't look across systems to find the best doctors and best prices. At their essence, ACOs are anti-competitive. They smother or absorb new entrants into the market.

In contrast, the payer revolt at the grassroots level has created a disruptive business model for the delivery of health care that encourages competition and choice and delivers lower costs. It had to happen, because the old business model has failed miserably. Its time has passed.

The reinvented model is patient-centric versus the impersonal, production-centric model. It is long term in scope, philosophy, and patient concern versus short term.

Reform Happening, but More Needed

This payer-led reform, racing ahead in the private economy, by no means denigrates the honest attempts at internal reform in the health care industry. Internal reform, such as the introduction of lean disciplines into hospitals and clinics, is absolutely necessary. But it is the external pressure from payers—employers and consumers—that is absolutely essential if broad-scale transformation is going to happen in American medicine.

Consider similar dynamics in another failing model in an equally important sector, that of increasingly unaffordable higher education. Students—especially nontraditional students, who are older, more demanding adults—don't want traditional four-year pathways that load them with debt. Budget-strapped students take less costly online courses, insist on credits for what they already know, and often opt for more flexible for-profit schools. Outside pressure is changing the game dramatically in higher education.

Consumers and innovators are also ripping up the old game plans in sectors like publishing, manufacturing, retail, banking, and agriculture. The new business models create pain and challenge for existing vendors, but serve the customer well. They reward innovators. So be it.

In health care, the payer revolt will reward providers who change their ways to meet the new market demands, and it will punish those who don't. The innovators will gain market share; the change-resistant laggards will fall back or go away.

In health care, the payer revolt will reward providers who change their ways to meet the new market demands, and it will punish those who don't. The innovators will gain market share; the change-resistant laggards will fall back or go away.

Hospital corporations stuck in the status quo face a double whammy. The volume fairy is going away. If they drop prices to keep volume without corresponding reductions in costs, their margins will take a hit. As all business-people know, marginal sales on the top line have a disproportionate impact on the bottom line, positive or negative.

Technology breakthroughs will also accelerate transformation. People will monitor their vital metrics with mobile devices. Geneticists will achieve predictive models so diseases can be discovered early and guarded against. Big databases will be mined to put more diagnostic tools in the hands of scarce primary care doctors. Telemedicine via smartphones will make some care more efficient.

In the past several decades, however, expensive new technologies have had the opposite result. MRI and CT scanners, while marvelous in terms of diagnosis, have proved to sharply increase the cost of care. They are often overutilized, and the high prices of scans bear no relation to their underlying costs. They have been a driver of bloated bills.

In every other economic sector, the introduction of new technology serves to improve performance and lower costs. Why not in health care?

The answer lies in the undisciplined business model that prevails. There is too little pressure to use technology to lower costs and prices. So, once again, it is the emerging marketplace that will drive transformation the most.

Ken Kaufman, a consultant to hospital corporations, warns their executives, "Provider revenues will be under severe pressure as payment mechanisms migrate toward value-based approaches. You need to do more with less." He urges hospital systems to convert to fee-for-value instead of fee-for-service.

WORLD CHANGING FOR INSURANCE COMPANIES

The disruptive business model racing across the private sector like a prairie fire will also have heavy impact on the health insurance industry.

Health insurers, the ultimate middlemen, are being "disintermediated" in two ways. As private companies move rapidly to self-insurance, the insurers are out of the risk-underwriting business. They will still reinsure the stop-loss insurance but not the bulk of the insurance claims.

Secondly, their role as middleman in arranging discounted networks will be undercut as providers offer fixed (nondiscounted) prices to corporate purchasers of care.

If hospitals and doctors put bundled prices out there for everyone to see on transparency websites, what's the need for highly variable discounts?

The new business model will cut many ways.

RACE TOWARD UNIVERSAL HEALTH CARE?

As for the great debate on universal access, the general direction of ObamaCare, it's a noble goal. But the nation can't afford unmanaged universal health care. Conversely, it should be achievable with a better economic model for care. The missing dimension in the new federal program is management, particularly behavior management.

The missing dimension in the new federal program is management, particularly behavior management.

We will see how this far-reaching law plays out. There are positive and negative predictions aplenty. The pioneer pilots for lowering costs did not yield expected results.

Fortunately, we don't have to guess how the grassroots revolution for improved health care will play out in the private sector. We know.

We know because the new business model for the delivery of health care has been developed empirically at the grassroots level. The private sector model has been built from the ground up. Each piece has been tested for results. The platforms and moving parts were fit into place only after they proved to work in the real world.

They have been analyzed and audited. They are beyond debate.

PRIVATE SECTOR HAS BROUGHT COSTS DOWN

In putting together the reengineered business model, the innovative private payers and the collaborating vendors in their medical supply chains are giving the nation a large gift. In truth, the health care industry alone can't be expected to fix the broken system.

Together with innovative payers, though, they are solving what is perhaps the nation's largest unsolved economic problem. Their solution is not a patch job, because it has the virtue of being rooted in enduring principles:

- **Individual responsibility.** It asks people to engage as responsible adults in attending to the long-term physical and financial health of their families.
- **Marketplace disciplines.** It installs consumerism front and center into the quest for best quality and prices. It steers volume to the high-value providers. That is real payment reform: do good work and you get the business.

- **Proactive care.** Instead of "sick care" that relishes "heads in beds," the new model keeps people healthier and out of hospitals.
- **Sound management.** It puts payers—employers and employees—back in charge of the medical supply chain.

There is every reason to believe that the grassroots reforms will bring order to the chaos on the economic side of health care. Indeed, if enough private sector managers engage the issue, there is even reason to believe that deflation in prices of health care could result. With three-times variation in pricing, rationalization offers huge savings.

The national bill for health care is so swollen at projections of nearly $3 trillion that aggressive management of the long-term trends could very well reverse and move toward lower expenditures, at least on a per capita basis.

The highest value providers are already there with prices at 20 percent to 30 percent below market averages. They just need to get a bigger slice of the business spend on health care for deflation to happen.

Note that the inflation beast has already been partially tamed. Double-digit hyperinflation was the pattern in the 1990s and into the next decade. Now the increases are in the 4 percent to 6 percent range.

What happened? The Great Recession certainly curbed health care spending from 2007 to 2009. But the trend continues downward, four years after the recession ended. And it is happening in the face of a graying population.

THE SERIGRAPH PRESCRIPTION

Serigraph's battle to tame its runaway health costs began a decade ago when it was facing a 15 percent increase in 2004. Since then, it has kept its total costs for medical, drug, and dental treatments to an average increase of less than 3 percent per year.

The company's benefits managers sought out innovators across the country and adapted their game-changing programs into its benefits plan for 500 employees and their families. Here are some pages out of our playbook:

- Self-insurance with a stop-loss of $200,000 per episode of care
- A consumer-driven plan with high-deductible options and a Health Reimbursement Account
- Full transparency on prices; partial on quality
- Free generic drugs
- Free prevention and wellness programs
- Free on-site clinic, including concierge doctors, nurse practitioner, health coach, dietician, and chiropractor
- Intense management of chronic diseases, including mental illness
- Management dashboards for workforce health and health expenses
- Centers of Value for procedures beyond primary care; employees receive incentives up to $2,000 or free surgeries for using the centers
- Required annual health risk assessments for physical and mental health, with follow-up coaching sessions
- Individual health plans
- Free counseling for Advance Directives
- Free hospice

It is the private sector payers who are bending the curve. One of the beauties of a marketplace is that it rewards innovation. Far-sighted employers are already being rewarded with healthier workforces and more affordable health benefits. The high-value health care providers are being rewarded with more business. And entrepreneurs are making big money by reinventing the sorry old model.

If the public sector follows the private sector into the real reforms, by no means a sure thing, taxpayers could catch a break, too.

Acknowledgments

THIS BOOK HAS MANY AUTHORS. They are the innovators across the country, many quoted in this book, who have led the way toward a disruptive new business model for health care in America. They are writing the playbook for the new game plan. There are many moving parts in the more workable more affordable model, and it takes bold change agents to fashion those parts. Collectively, they have positioned their organizations and the country for better health and lower costs of care.

In crafting the manuscript itself, my particular gratitude goes to my wife, Kine, my most stern copy editor; Sheila Goehring, who produced and deciphered the manuscript; Michele Derus, able journalist; Jon Rauser, reliable broker and source; David Kracht, Scott Fuller, and Jo Thompson, my company's benefits consultants; Linda Buntrock, who executes Serigraph's innovations; and my brother Tom, a sage editor. They made sure I stayed on solid ground while stitching together what's happening at the grassroots level to transform the economic realities of health care.

.

About Serigraph

SERIGRAPH INC. is a mid-size manufacturer of decorative parts with about 600 co-workers in West Bend, Wisconsin. It makes products like the face of the instrument cluster in a car, the control console of a clothes washer, and the menu board in a quick-service restaurant. The company also has plants in Mexico and India, where health costs are largely borne by the governments. In West Bend, Serigraph and its co-workers spend about $9,000 per employee on health care, split about 80/20 percent between employer and employee. The company's health plan offers a full range of medical, drug, and dental benefits. Employee surveys rank the health plan on top of all aspects of the company.